LIVING A RICH LIFE

The No-Regrets Guide to Building and Spending Wealth

James M. Lenhoff with G.E. Williams

Cover design by Wendy Bentley, www.wendybentleydesign.com
Front cover photo: Langarion/Shutterstock

Printed in the United States of America

Second Edition, First Printing, 2018

ISBN: 978-1-945091-87-2

Library of Congress Control Number: 2018952392

Ordering information: Special discounts are available on quantity purchases by bookstores, corporations, associations, and others. For details, contact the publisher at:

sales@braughlerbooks.com
or at 937-58-BOOKS

For questions or comments about this book, please write to:

info@braughlerbooks.com

Braughler™
Books
braughlerbooks.com

Contents

Contents

Introduction

When I began writing this book, the working title was simply Money and Regret. My marketing-savvy friends told me that the title felt a bit negative, and didn't really capture all that I wanted to *accomplish* in the book. I agree, but there is a central truth in that working title that I want you to get before reading this book: Over time, both money and regret compound exponentially.

Let me give you an example of what I mean. One day, I was meeting with a client who was 83 years old. He was worth multiple millions of dollars, simply because when he got his first job, he had developed the habit of putting a small amount of money aside from each paycheck. There is a trajectory of building wealth that is pretty easy to map out when someone does that. Just a little bit of money put aside every month, over time, can create a fortune far out of proportion to each individual investment. It's the power of compounding interest. Money creates more money all by itself. It's breathtaking.

But do you know what we talked about in that meeting? We talked about regret. We talked about how always chasing the next bonus and the next raise and the next promotion had replaced the time he wished he'd spent with his wife and children. We talked about vacations that they went on without him, because he couldn't possibly miss work. We talked about how he now felt like a stranger in his own family, and how he would give up his entire fortune if he could go back and make different decisions.

A few days later, I was talking with another client. This one was in his early 30s. He told me how disappointed he was that he had to miss his daughter's first ballet recital, but he was leading a major project at work that was going to put him in line for the next promotion. And that was when I realized that regret has its own trajectory. I had clients who were making the same sorts of decisions at every age and stage in life, and I could see the slow, steady arc of progression from this young man just starting out to the heartbroken eighty-three-year-old man I'd met with a few days earlier. Over time, decisions that seem small can create a mass of regret way out of proportion to each individual decision. It's the power of compounding regret. Regret creates more regret all by itself. It's heartbreaking.

That was the day I decided it wasn't my job just to help people build big fortunes. My real job was to help people accumulate wealth without accumulating regret.

I didn't just want to help people get rich; I wanted to help them lead rich lives. So I became a student of regret and all that it had to teach me about what matters in life. I want to share what I've learned with you in this book, not so that you can just build wealth, but so that you can build wealth while living a rich life.

CHAPTER 1

Don't Make Decisions out of Worry

You should be worried. Very worried.

At least, that's the impression you'll get if you pay attention to the network financial news. And here is why: fear is the most powerful marketing tool that exists. It is the surest way to get people's attention, at least in the short-term. It is the most reliable method to get viewers to stay tuned or get website visitors to click-through. And since the news giants depend on viewers and visits to drive their advertising dollars, many of them shamelessly and ceaselessly use fear to hook you.

Here's how it works. Tune into most of the higher rated financial news shows, and you will see talking heads telling you how bad things are about to get. Their message is this:

Everything is going to fall apart, and you should be worried that you are going to go down with the ship. Get out now before it's too late!

The details of the story will change from one expert to another. One will tell you that everything is about to fall apart because the Fed lowered (or raised) the interest rate too much, and the next expert will say everything is about to go south because the Fed didn't lower (or raise) the interest rate enough. Keep watching and more experts follow, each with their own insight as to why you should be worried: A rise (or decrease) in unemployment, an increase (or decrease) in new housing construction, or the weakening (or strengthening) of the dollar all have hidden ripple effects that could wipe out your retirement account. Political problems in South America, military problems in Asia, or banking problems in Europe are all trotted out as potential triggers for a worldwide economic catastrophe. The dominoes are falling, and they are headed straight towards your bank and your money. You should be worried. *Very* worried.

But here's the fun part. The networks also get to play the opposite side of the fear coin to get your attention. In between the talking heads telling you how bad things are about to get are other talking heads telling you how good things are about to get. Their message is this:

Something is about to explode with growth, and you should be worried that you are going to miss out on the opportunity of a lifetime. Get in now before it's too late!

These experts can sound just as convincing as the experts who tell you that everything is falling apart. Sometimes they will use the exact same circumstances as doomsday experts, but will portray them instead as opportunities to amass a great fortune as long as you invest heavily in gold, or foreign markets, or clean energy. The unemployment rate that is the signal for implosion to one analyst is the signal for tremendous upside to another analyst. Sometimes, they will talk about a new technology, or a medical innovation, or a new shift in the way consumers are making purchasing decisions, with the promise that if you are one of the discerning few who understand how revolutionary this is, you could become rich beyond your wildest imaginations. But if you blink, the opportunity will evaporate and you will be left with dreams of what could have been. You should be worried. Very worried.

And here's where the fear factory really kicks into high gear. Not only are we told how things are going to fall apart, or how we might miss our only chance to get rich, we are told this all day, every day. There was a time when you could get everything you needed to know to be well-informed by spending 30 minutes with Walter Cronkite. That 30 minutes included domestic and international news, politics, science and technology, updates on the war, and perhaps a minute or two on the economy. 30 minutes and you could lay your head on the pillow that night with the confidence that you were a well-informed adult. Not anymore. Today, there is a non-stop torrent of news coming your way. What about the stories you didn't read? What about the experts you didn't get a chance to listen to? You could be missing vital information. And how does all this information fit together? Which stories are the most important? Isn't it ironic that one of the results of the explosion of news is that we feel less capable of making informed decisions?

And our anxiety about making informed decisions is only increased by how exaggerated the news has become. To get our attention, they speak in the superlative. The market wasn't just down — it was the worst day in three weeks. The market wasn't up — it was the best two-day run since last month. This reporting of everyday, mundane news in extreme language is designed to amplify our anxiety and arrest our attention.

The supposed importance of these news items is further inflated by the way they are over-reported. What Walter Cronkite spent five minutes on, today's news shows spend five days on. Five days! Walter Cronkite didn't spend five days on the moon landing! But today we always seem to be in the middle of some historic crisis, with a barrage of coverage, the same video clip from every angle and every talking head's expert opinion –inflating and exaggerating the importance of this one news item. Then, suddenly, this item that was so critical is dropped and forgotten when the next historic event happens and we go through the same cycle.

Make no mistake: The networks know that their greatest tool in getting your attention is anxiety, and they have become experts at creating and sustaining this anxiety. I'm convinced that when historians look back at this period of time, they will call it The Age of Worry.

Imagine, for just a moment, if they told the truth. Imagine seeing this:

> *Tonight's headline: Everything is fluctuating up and down just about the same way it always has and always will, and while it is all very interesting for those of us who like that sort of thing, over the long run it will have little impact on you and your financial security.*

If you saw that headline you probably wouldn't be compelled to keep watching, or to click and read the article. So, we can understand why the news outlets use fear to get our attention. It's good for business. But it doesn't mean we have to fall for it. It doesn't mean we have to park ourselves curbside for the unending parade of fear. And yet, sadly, many do just that. I've noticed that the people who are most fixated on watching the financial news channels are also the ones who have the most anxiety about their money. I often joke with clients that the twenty-four hour news cycle could be the beginning of the downfall of civilization.

Keep Calm and Carry On

The economic world is very complex, and that's a good thing. In fact, one of the reasons why we don't have to overreact to any new bump in the financial road is because it's so complex. In technical terms, we would refer to this by saying the economy has high causal density. Let me explain what that means, because it's very helpful in reducing anxiety.

Imagine a head of a pin that has a thousand different forces acting on it from every direction, and suddenly it moves slightly to the right. Now imagine you had to diagnose why it moved that way. It would be impossible, because there are too many forces to account for, all interacting on one another and on the head of the pin. That is what our economy is like. Every day, there are thousands of economic forces pushing and pulling, squeezing and twisting, lifting and restraining to get the end result of the Dow Jones closing three points higher or twenty points lower. That's high causal density.

Now, here is why knowing this can protect you from worry. The next time you hear an expert predicting a financial doomsday, notice what they are doing. They will take one factor out of the thousands of factors impacting the economy, and will say, in effect, "I know without a shadow of a doubt which force on the head of the pin is making it move. In fact, this one force is so important it is going to move the pin all by itself." The next time you hear something like that, you will know that for what they say to be true, every other economic force would have to literally disappear — and that's not going to happen.

So here is the situation we find ourselves in. We live in a time when many of our sources for financial news use anxiety to draw us in and keep us hooked, even though making financial decisions based on worry will lead to some of the biggest regrets of our lives. To understand why this is so, let's think about how worrying works.

The Nature of Worry

Imagine that you are driving down a beautiful country road. You glance at your dashboard and the fuel gauge needle is on empty. Yikes! You are about to run out of gas. You do a search on your phone and discover that the closest gas station is ten miles ahead. You don't know how long your gauge has been on empty, so you're not sure how far you can go before the car sputters to a stop. Now you have two choices. You can relax and enjoy the beautiful country scenery until you reach the gas station or run out of gas; or, you can worry, imagining all the terrible things that could happen, until you reach the gas station or run out of gas. So here's the question: How much farther will the remaining gas take you if you choose to worry instead of choosing to relax and enjoy the ride?

Not an inch farther. The only thing worrying will do is steal away the time you could have spent enjoying the ride. And let's say just for the sake of argument that you do run out of gas after nine miles. After all, sometimes things go wrong in life. Now you're stuck on the side of the road, and you will either have to call for help or hike the mile to the gas station. So here's the question: How much easier will it be to dial that number or hike that mile if you spent the last nine miles worrying instead of enjoying the ride?

Not a bit easier.

But what if you are an expert worrier, the kind of worrier who believes that avoiding problems is the most important thing in life? If you are an expert worrier, you know exactly what to do: you pull off the road and turn off the engine! Problem solved. There's no way you're going to run out of gas now! But there is also no way you are going to get where you want to go. And, again, here's the question: When, after ten minutes or ten hours or ten years, you finally get tired of being stuck and decide to get back on the road, how much farther will the remaining gas take you because you spent that time frozen in fear?

Not a bit further.

There have been many things that people have said in history about the nature of worry. One of my favorites is from the Bible, where Jesus says:

Who of you by worrying can add a single hour to your life?

The answer, of course, is none of us can. Not a single hour. And this is the nature of worry. It can be all-consuming, but in the end it accomplishes nothing. It steals our time, it steals our enjoyment of life, and it causes us to make really bad financial decisions.

Just like Lloyd and Jane, who were very worried about their money. Of course they were worried; they had one of the major financial news channels running in their home almost non-stop. Every time they called me, I could hear it in the background. One day, they came in to see me, telling me that they had some major concerns that they needed to discuss. It turned out that they had been listening to one of the doomsday scenarios and were convinced that they needed to move all of their investments into cash to escape the looming stock market crash.

I tried to talk them off the ledge. I knew their decision was coming out of a place of worry, and that worry always leads to regret. I let them know that, yes, sometimes the stock market goes down in the short term, and sometimes the stock market goes up in the short term. But they could still have confidence in their financial plan. I reminded them that they were invested in a balanced portfolio that would serve to smooth out the market's volatility over time and help them accomplish their goals. The best thing they could do was to continue to stay the course. But they wouldn't be persuaded and still insisted that I move all of their investments into cash. So what else could I do? After all, I worked for them.

So I refused.

I must admit that was a bit of a shock to them, and they demanded an explanation. I walked them through the alternatives.

"Look," I said, "to achieve your current goals, you need a 6% return on your investment. With the investments you have now, you have an extremely high likelihood of success. Over the long term, you can have confidence that this will be the case no matter what happens in the short term. Now, what happens if you move everything to cash? You guarantee a 0% rate of return. Why would you choose the alternative that is guaranteed to fail?"

In the end, they couldn't be dissuaded and I resigned as their advisor. They hired someone who was happy to follow their anxiety-produced strategy. Over the next two years, the crash they had prophesied never occurred. The stock market continued to climb slowly but surely. By the time they admitted their mistake, they had lost the opportunity to add hundreds of thousands of dollars to their net worth.

Here is the worst part about worry. It not only leads us to make bad decisions, but the impact of those decisions compound over time. When we allow worry to become a part of our lives, panicked decisions lead to even more panicked decisions.

The Nature of Worry: Part 2

Imagine for a moment that you are at the grocery store and there are three long lines. You get in the shortest line, but soon notice that the line next to you is going faster. You're worried that you might have chosen the wrong line, so you get out of your line and go to the back of the faster line.

Two customers ahead of you are served pretty quickly, but then the third customer argues about the price of the cottage cheese. The cashier calls the manager over and they look through this week's circular and can't find the sale price the customer swears is there. They call a bagger over and ask him to run to the dairy section to see what the price of the cottage cheese is there. You've already lost three minutes, and realize it's going to take another few minutes for the bagger to complete his quest. Once again, you are worried that you chose the wrong line, so you get out of that line, and move towards the back of the first line, which is now moving faster.

Now, a lady with two full carts of groceries and a box full of coupons slides into the line just before you and you can only imagine how long she will take to check out, so you opt for line number three.

Line three is humming, so you begin to calm down. After a few customers, it's shift change time for the cashiers, so it takes about a minute for the outgoing cashier to get her drawer and paperwork together and for the new cashier to get logged in. A minute is not that bad, so you stay where you are. Then you notice that the new cashier is a talker. She likes to talk to her customers. A lot. And she is in no hurry ring up orders. As you think about changing lines yet again, you notice that the person who was behind you when you first entered line one has just finished paying and is walking out the door.

Panicked decisions lead to more panicked decisions.

Remember Lloyd and Jane? After two years of losing out on growing their wealth they began to panic again, and decided to re-enter the stock-market — just as it was about to crest and enter a downturn. This was a very natural cycle for the stock-market, but Lloyd and Jane were getting in at the back of the line.

This is another way that decisions based on worry compound over time. By the time we are willing to admit our mistakes we are simply setting ourselves up for a brand new mistake, *and the new mistake only confirms the thinking that led to the first mistake.* When Lloyd and Jane watched the market go up and up and up and finally admitted they had made a mistake by going to cash, they got back into the market just as it was about to go down. What was their response? Did they see how one decision based on worry led to another decision based on worry? No. Their response was, "See! We were right all along! We *knew* the market was going to go down!" The second mistake just confirmed their bias that they should be very worried about their money.

That's what worry does. It causes us to make panicked decisions to solve problems that don't exist and then learn the wrong lesson. When I first started out as a financial advisor, I noticed that whenever there was a bump in the economy, I would get calls from lots of worried clients: What does this bump mean? Do I need to completely change my investment strategy? Am I in danger of losing everything? Here was the interesting part: Though I would get lots of calls from lots of worried clients, I wouldn't get any calls from my wealthiest clients. I reached a conclusion:

The people with the biggest fortunes don't have to worry.

Now I know I was wrong. After years of watching the interaction between worry and wealth-building, I know that the converse is true:

The people who don't worry build the biggest fortunes. Big worry and big regrets

I once had a client named Henry, though I usually think of him as Used-to-Be Henry. That's because Henry always talked about his life in the past tense. He used to be a huge Shakespeare fan. He used to love classic Corvettes. He used to really be into protecting the environment. He used to be fanatical about Major League Baseball. He used to be passionate about reversing urban decay and helping the poor.

Whenever we got together to go over his finances, I would assure Henry that he was on track with all of his financial goals. I wanted to know what he planned on doing with his extra money. How about a trip to England to see Hamlet at the Globe Theatre? What about taking a couple of weeks and doing a baseball road trip, visiting five or six different ball parks? What about looking for your dream Corvette? What about making a contribution to the World Wildlife Fund or donating computers to an inner-city school? I was interested in learning how he was going to use his extra money in a way that made his life more meaningful and enjoyable.

But Henry was a worrier. For Henry, there was always a potential crisis around the next corner. He wasn't exactly sure when or how it would come, but he was always on high alert. He convinced himself that he couldn't afford to do anything in life that he loved, because he would probably need that money to survive the coming calamity. I began to realize that the reason he spoke about his life in the past tense is because Henry was no longer living; he was merely surviving. When Henry retired and was no longer bringing home a paycheck, he went into survival mode. His only goal was to protect the assets he had accumulated.

So I scaled back my suggestions, hoping to fan into flames any spark that was left of the person who used to be Henry. Instead of going to England, how about purchasing a season subscription to the local Shakespeare Company? Instead of taking a baseball road trip, what about taking your family to see a game when your favorite team comes to town? What about making a small donation to a cause you care about? How about spending a day at the Corvette Museum?

But Henry wasn't biting. He was sure even these small expenditures would ruin him.

Redeeming Worry

Then something happened that changed Henry. His wife was diagnosed with an aggressive cancer and died a short time later. Henry realized that of all the things that he was worried about, this wasn't even on the list — he never saw it coming. He also realized that even if he had seen it coming, he couldn't have stopped it. He began to see how useless his worry had been. Henry decided it was time to get out of survival mode and start living again, while he still had the chance.

Henry came back to life. He took his son and grandson on a baseball road trip, a trip that his grandson still talks about as one of the highlights of his life. He bought an old Corvette and enjoyed hours upon hours in the garage restoring it. He thought about going to London, but decided he would be just as happy with a season subscription to the local Shakespeare Company. He started making regular contributions to the causes that he cared about, which led to getting more involved in the causes he cared about. And, since he was still following a sound financial plan, he didn't run out of money. There was more than enough.

Guarding against worry

It would be nice to never worry, but for most of us, worry is a common reaction to life's uncertainties and complexities. If we want to ensure that we are not going to make financial decisions based on worry, we need a way to deal with our worry when it arises. I help my clients guard against worry by asking two simple questions.

The first question is, What is the thought that is behind the worry? Beneath the emotional experience of worry is always a thought. Often, these thoughts are vague and undefined. We get so caught up in the emotional experience of worrying that we don't take the time to surface the belief that lies beneath the worry. When we surface the thought, it will sound something like this:

I'm worried because if I let this opportunity pass me by, I will never have another opportunity like it.

I'm worried because the market has gone down 3%, and I'm probably going to lose all my money.

I'm worried because I'll never have enough for retirement.

Once we have surfaced and clarified the thought that is causing us to worry, we can ask the question that we almost never ask when worry controls our decisions: Is that thought true?

Is it true that I will never have another opportunity?

Is it true that I am going to lose all my money?

Is it true that I will never have enough for retirement?

This is one of the most powerful things about having a financial plan. It helps you to answer the Is that thought true? question, which helps you not waste time worrying. If you don't have a financial plan, then it can be difficult to answer whether you will have enough for retirement, so the worry attached to that belief is hard to escape. But if you have a plan, it's much simpler. When I meet a client who is worried about running out of money, I ask a couple simple questions.

"Are you spending more money than what we planned?" "No."

"Are you making less money than what we planned?" "No."

"Well then, according to the math is the thought, I'm going to run out of money, true? "No."

A solid financial plan makes answering the Is that thought true? question quick and easy, and allows you to get back to enjoying life. Perhaps you have been worried about your financial situation. Maybe you are worried that you have already made too many poor financial decisions and that your current financial situation is so bad you'll never be able to turn it around. Maybe you are worried that you have waited too long to start investing for retirement. Maybe you have been doing fairly well, but you still worry about whether or not you have enough to feel secure and start enjoying life.

If that sounds like you, I've got some good news. You don't have to be a slave to worry.

Time and time again, I meet with clients for the first time, and the emotions that they are experiencing at the beginning of the meeting are worry, fear, confusion, anxiety, and a sense of being overwhelmed. We'll spend that first meeting getting a clear picture of their current financial reality, get clarity about where they are trying to get to in life, and begin designing a path to help them get there. Despite how good or how bad their current situation is, when they leave at the end of the meeting, their emotions towards their financial world have transformed. Instead of fear and anxiety, they are experiencing confidence, hope, clarity and a sense of comfort in their current financial reality.

That's in one meeting.

When that first meeting ends, here is the sentence I hear almost every time:

I wish we would have done this sooner!

Why? Because, it is a life-transforming experience to learn that you don't have to worry about your money.

My hope is that as you read this book, you will experience that transformation from worrying about your finances to becoming confident in your ability to build and spend wealth in ways that create a great life for you and the people you love. Perhaps, like the driver with the gas gauge on empty, you pulled over to the side of the road and turned off your engine a long time ago. I want to help you get back on the road to where you want to get in life, and I want to help you enjoy every mile of the journey.

CHAPTER 2

Don't Trade Relationships for Money

I recently had lunch with Mike, a friend who retired a few years ago after a very successful career with a multinational consumer goods company. His job had allowed him to travel the world and he had become well-known and well-respected in his industry.

"Have you started writing your memoirs yet?" I asked, only half joking. Mike was a great storyteller, and I always loved hearing about the far-flung places he had been and the many business and leadership challenges he had overcome.

Mike became surprisingly somber.

"If I were to write my memoirs," he said, "I would call them *The Man Who was Never There.*"

I wasn't sure where he was going with this, so I waited for him to continue.

"Retirement has been a bit of surprise for me," he said after a few quiet moments. "I always assumed it would be a chance to spend a lot of time with Chrissy and the girls. I always thought that after sacrificing so much to provide for them over the course of my career, retirement would be my reward. I thought we would have lots of fun together."

He had my complete attention. Mike is one of the most honest, authentic men I know. He has always allowed me to learn from his life's lessons, whether they came from his successes or from his failures.

"What I've learned," he continued, "is that my family spent the last 40 years learning how to live without me. They didn't have a choice. I was never there. Not at the important stuff, and not at the little stuff. Never. I know they appreciate me. I'm pretty sure they love me. But when I get together with my daughters, it's awkward. Not what I dreamed of."

"You know," he said, "I was almost tempted to go back to work, just to avoid the awkwardness. But then I realized that I would just be making the same mistake all over again. So, I'm going to keep doing what it takes to rebuild a connection with my family while I still have a chance."

As a financial advisor, I've had the opportunity to see how people live out their retirement years, and here's the tragedy: people don't become the person who was never there because they are horrible, selfish people who don't care about their spouses or children or friends. I've met many men and women who ended their careers much like Mike, and in almost every case, they are heartbroken and filled with deep regret. They are usually good, unselfish, and even sacrificial people who weren't aware of the two powerful forces pulling them away from the people that they love. I call these forces the Lure and the Lie.

The Lure and the Lie

If you want to live a life that is rich and meaningful, and if you want to avoid building up regret, here is the single most important thing you can do:

Stop trading relationships for money.

None of us sets out in life to become the man or the woman who was never there, to end our careers with lots of money and possessions, only to find that the people who are most important to us are cold, distant, or even resentful. And yet — and please pay attention to this, because it is the second most important sentence in this chapter — it is frighteningly easy to become the person who was never there. That's because there are two forces at work in your life every day that are trying to pull you away from the people that matter most to you. There are two forces that will make it easy to trade relationship for money.

How can that be? Well, just remember what it was like the first time you spent a day at the beach and experienced a phenomenon called longshore drift. Picture yourself back on your favorite stretch of shoreline. You claim your spot and set up your towel, beach chair, and umbrella. You lug out your cooler of cold drinks and snacks and place it next to your towel. You put on your sunscreen, and now you're ready for some fun in the ocean. So you hit the waves and for the next hour, it's like you're a kid again. You body surf, you crash into the waves, you feel the sand churning back and forth around your feet, and you bob up and down with the rhythm of the ocean. Then you look up, and your towel and umbrella are nowhere in sight. You find that, even though you never once swam to the left or the right, you are now hundreds of feet away from where you began. That's the power of longshore drift. You don't have to try to drift away from where you wanted to be, because there are invisible forces at work that will do it for you. Now imagine that as you are drifting down the shoreline, you reach a point where the ocean looks calm. The waves aren't breaking and the surface of the water is flat and serene. It doesn't take long to discover that what appeared peaceful is actually another powerful, invisible force — a rip current. This rip current is now sweeping you out to sea with all the force of a rushing river. Once again, you don't have to do anything to get swept out to deep water. Longshore drift and rip currents will happen without any effort on your part, just like the two invisible forces at work in your career.

The first force is the lure of more, and it is a force that will be acting on you throughout your career. Work just a little longer and you can have more money. Give up just a little more of your time with your family and you can have more power, a bigger office, a more prestigious title, and a greater reputation among your colleagues.

Each time you climb the corporate ladder, you are not only rewarded with more, you are once again tempted by the lure of even more. At first, you're not even aware that your new position will require you to sacrifice time with your family. "You won't have to travel that often," you hear. The message from your employer is clear: You can have it all. That turns into spending a week every month away from home. Soon, you get used to the extra money and the perks and the time away, and it starts to feel normal. Now that you have reached this level, it will take only a little more sacrifice to reach the next level. Just a few more hours away from the people you love and you can add profit sharing and a bigger pension to your pile of more. And make no mistake, more can be nice. One of the great things about having more is that it allows us to have even more. More money means more luxurious cars, more expensive vacations, and bigger houses. It means our kids can go to more expensive colleges.

And the lure of more never ends. There is always another raise, a bigger promotion, or a more prestigious title. You can become CEO of your company and still, the lure of more will entice you with the opportunity to become the CEO of a bigger company. A reporter once asked John D. Rockefeller, the founder of Standard Oil and one of the world's first billionaires, how much money was enough. His answer: "just a little bit more." Rockefeller understood that more is never enough. More is an ever-present force that, if you are not paying attention, will cause you to drift far away from your family and friends. More will entice you to trade relationships for money. Just like the drift at the shoreline, all you have to do is let it take you.

As much as they love you, there is nothing that the people who matter most to you can do to compete with the lure of more. Your children can't give you a raise if you spend just a little bit more time helping them with their homework, or helping them discover how they are uniquely wired, or helping them feel strong and connected to you as they face life's challenges. Your spouse can't give you a promotion if you become just a little more competent at listening, or if you spend just a little more time each day doing the little things that make him or her feel known and loved.

To be clear, I'm not saying that we always need to be there for our spouse or children or friends. We need to model to our children that work costs something, and so we cannot be at every baseball practice or coach every soccer game. What I am saying is that between the two extremes of being the person who was always there and being the person who was never there, there is a powerful, invisible, and ever-present force that will pull you towards becoming the person who was never there. And that's just one of the forces.

The second force is the lie of being irreplaceable, and if you are not aware of it this lie will become a rip current that will pull you far away from the people and things that matter most to you. The lie goes like this: You are the only one who can do this job, or meet this deadline, or lead this project, or land this account. Your work is indispensable to your department, or your school, or your hospital. If you don't do whatever it takes to succeed, everything is going to fall apart. It all rests on your shoulders. When we believe the lie, we become superheroes, larger-than-life figures on whom everything depends. Since everything depends on us, it's only natural that our company asks us to sacrifice more for the cause.

Let's be honest: it can be intoxicating. We get a sense of our own importance, we get recognition and praise, and we get awards and rewards for being the only person who could possibly have accomplished what we have accomplished. Just like the lure of more, the lie of being irreplaceable never ends. After each accomplishment, there is another challenge where our supervisors or administrators or board are convinced that we are the only ones who can deliver the goods. Once again, we saddle-up, ready to sacrifice for the heroic cause.

What happens if you believe the lie? What happens if you spend your life as the superhero at work, always sacrificing whatever it takes to accomplish the next goal, charged up by the promise that you are indispensable? I'll tell you what happens, because I've heard the story over and over again: On your last day of work, there will be a cake and a funny Hallmark card in the conference room, and you will get a handshake and a pat on the back as you walk out the door. The next day, there will be a hundred people standing in line to get your job, people who are driven by the same lure of more and the same lie of being irreplaceable. One of them will be chosen as your successor, and the machine will drone on, and no one will miss you.

It will be like you were never there.

And then you go home and discover that your spouse and children really don't know you. Just like Mike's daughters, they've learned to live without you — not by choice, but as a matter of necessity. And you really don't know who they are or how to become a part of their lives again. Everything feels awkward, and you realize that you have decades of catching up to do. Where do you begin?

There are places in your universe where you truly are irreplaceable, where you truly are the one and only person who can fill that role. You are your spouse's only husband or wife. You are your children's only father or mother. You are the only oldest sister or youngest brother that your siblings will ever know. If you abandon your responsibility in these relationships, it will cause a real void in the lives of the people who matter most to you, a void that no one else on the planet can fill. And once again, there is no way the people that love you the most can compete with the lie of being irreplaceable. There are two main reasons for this.

Reason number one: to be honest, it's not intoxicating. Even when you are the best spouse or parent in the world, it's still not intoxicating. Your kids are not constantly rewarding you with praise for the efforts you are making at being a good parent, and your spouse will never host an awards banquet for you and invite all your friends. Your ego will rarely get fed, and the moments you feel like a superhero are few and far between.

Reason number two: to be even more honest, you're not the best spouse or parent in the world. You might have gone to school for six years to learn to excel at your profession, but like the rest of us, you were probably given a total of zero hours of training in how to be a great spouse. You might have gone through a meticulous and rigorous program from your company to ensure you had all the skills and information you needed to succeed, but like the rest of us you probably haven't been in a single training session on how to be an effective parent. Most of us have no idea what we are in for and we only learn by trial and error, with an extra helping of error. Is it any wonder that we are often tempted to ignore these roles where we feel so uncomfortable and instead spend time where we get our egos stroked for being so good at what we do?

The Lifestyle Cap

Because it is frighteningly easy to become the person who was never there, and because the Lure and the Lie will be ever-present, invisible forces seducing us to trade relationships for money, we need an opposing force that will anchor us to the things that really matter the most in life. I learned this the hard way.

It happened one day when I was driving to an appointment with a prospective client — a really good prospective client. I was young and committed to climbing the ladder. I was working eighty hours a week, skipping breakfast and lunch, stacking meeting after meeting. Whatever the challenge, I could make it work. My wife was pregnant, which was exciting, but I was never with her. I could make that work, though. I knew if I worked hard enough, I could make it all work. I glanced at my watch and I was fifteen minutes late. I was still twenty minutes away. Fifteen minutes late and twenty minutes away — how do I make that work? I started to feel a pressure in my chest. *This is an important client. If I mess this up, I'm screwed.* My heart was pounding against my chest. *How do I make it work when I'm fifteen minutes late and twenty minutes away?* Every minute that went by, the pressure doubled. Now I was having a full-on panic attack and I had to pull over and just breathe. Finally, I was able to call and cancel the appointment, and I lost the client. I was undone.

Reality came crashing down on me: I wasn't making it all work. I was just exhausting myself chasing something that I wasn't even sure that I wanted.

I didn't know it at the time, but I had succumbed to the Lure and the Lie. I realized that day that something had to change, which led to some very crucial conversations with my wife. We talked about what we wanted out of life and the kind of lifestyle that would make us truly happy. We also thought through how much it would cost to live that life. Then we talked about how much we needed to save, so that we could continue to live that life through our retirement years. Then we made the decision that has helped us to stay anchored to the people we love. *We decided since this is enough to live the life that we want to live, this is the spending cap we are setting on our lifestyle. We need this much to spend for today and this much to save for retirement. If we get more than what we have decided to spend and save, we will give it away.* And, since we've already decided that our Lifestyle Cap is what we *really want* out of life to be happy, it's very easy to live with. It's very freeing to know that you don't need more to be happy, and that you will never need more to be happy.

Since our Lifestyle Cap is so easy to live with, the Lure of more is not a problem; and since the Lifestyle Cap is created primarily to anchor me to the people I love, the Lie of being irreplaceable is not a problem.

Now, please don't read the term Lifestyle Cap and think that it means austerity. I'm in no way suggesting that you live a lifestyle that you believe to be harsh or barren. That wouldn't make you happy and that's not what I want for you. I want something different for you — and just in case you have been wondering and waiting, here is the most important sentence in this chapter:

I want you to recognize that the meaning of life is relationship.

We have been tricked into thinking that the meaning of life is to accumulate money, or that satisfaction in life comes from accumulating more and better stuff. We've been promised that fulfillment will come from having a certain title or degree or position.

I've been struck by how our birth and our death, the two great bookends of our life, are really good indicators of where meaning in life really comes from. What's happening at birth? We all know because it's one of the most fun and most meaningful experiences of life. A new baby is ushered into life and immediately begins bonding with her parents. Soon, this instant relationship expands to include siblings, grandparents, aunts and uncles, and close friends, who are all eager to hold her, nuzzle her, and celebrate her. Could anything be more filled with meaning than that?

What's happening at death? We don't all know because it's one of the scariest experiences in life and we try to avoid thinking about it. I've had enough clients who've reached that part of their life and I can tell you that no one wants to make sure they get one more ride in their Ferrari. No one wishes they had a bigger house. No, they want their children and their spouse and their family around them. It's the only thing they have left that they care about. All the things they thought they cared about, all the stuff they worried about and about which they kept meticulous records — it all goes out the window. And all they are trying to figure out is how to get their kids to spend some time with them before they die.

I want to save you the regret of getting to the end of your career and realizing that you traded the thing that was most important for something that is much less important, trading the only thing that can bring meaning and satisfaction to your life for something that will leave you empty.

I want your work to be full of purpose and dignity. I want your career to be a good thing. But I want you to also be aware there is a point at which it can become a very negative thing that damages, or even eliminates, the whole reason you are here. That's why there has to be very clear lines that we draw that say this much and no more. I will take my vacation because I need to invest in my family. I will work a reasonable number of hours a week because I need to be home with my kids.

People say to me all the time, "that's easy for you, because you're already successful." But I've been doing this from very early in my career. In fact, I'm not convinced that you have to choose between setting limits at work and being successful. When you are living a balanced life and you are engaged in deep relationship with your family, you are a better worker. I'm way more efficient because I go home and rest, enjoy my children, and have great conversations with my wife. When I get back to work, my tank is full and I'm ready to give my best because I'm at my best.

Two big questions

To create your Lifestyle Cap, you will need to have significant conversations with all of the stakeholders. That means your spouse if you are married and your children if you are a parent. Their opinion is important. In these conversations, you will need to come up with the answers to two big questions.

The first question is, What are our non-negotiables? There is no one-size-fits-all Lifestyle Cap, and I'm certainly not going to tell you what should or shouldn't make you content. Each one of us is unique, so each Lifestyle Cap is unique. For some, home schooling is a non-negotiable while for others, private schooling is a non-negotiable. For some families living on a single income is a non-negotiable and for others, it won't be a significant factor. For some, season tickets for the football team are non-negotiables, while others would be happy if they never watched another game in their life. For some, it will be important to have a house with a large back yard, while for others living in a condo is all they need. The key is taking the time to discover what is most important to you and the other people in your life.

The second question which you will need to answer is, What are the consequences of our non-negotiables? I was once helping some clients create their Lifestyle Cap and it was very clear that the wife was miserable because the husband traveled so much for work. She was lonely and was living the life of single parent. It became clear to them both that having a job that allowed him to be in town full-time was a non-negotiable. The husband was actually excited about the idea.

"I will have no problem finding a job that keeps me here," he said. "But what this means is we are going to have to move to a smaller house, and we will have to move our kids from private school to public school. It will probably also mean that we'll need to scale back how much money we spend on our vacations. But I'm sure it will be worth it in the long run." I could actually see life returning to his face as he was saying this. It was clear that all the time away from the family had taken its toll on him as well.

That's when we hit the snag. She didn't want to move to a smaller house, and she didn't want to take her kids out of private school. She didn't want to give up the trips to Hawaii and Italy

"Hmmm," he thought. "I guess what that means is that you are going to have to get a full-time job to pay for those things." At this point, she wasn't working outside the home because he traveled so much, and besides, he was making so much that she didn't need to. She didn't want that either.

Your non-negotiables always have consequences. Saying Yes to the things that are most important to you will mean that you will have to say No to some things that are good but are not as important. It can be a challenging process, but in the end, you will have a deeper understanding of who you are and what really makes you happy.

The wife just needed some time to understand herself and sort through what was really important to her. In the end, she realized that the big house and the private school were not critical to her happiness. They were nice, yes. And she was honest enough to admit that they did something for her ego, but she could live without that. On the other hand, she also realized that the expensive vacations were a non-negotiable for her. She loved the adventure of seeing new places, and sharing these adventures with her husband and children were always the highlight of her year. In the end, he found a great job in town and she worked ten hours a week, which covered their globe-trotting vacations.

Redeeming the Decisions to Trade Relationships for Money

Here's the irony: Most of the time, when we trade relationship for money, it is not because we are selfish people with toxic hearts. Most of the time, we do it out of a desire to give more to the people that we love. There is something that we believe we should be providing that we can't provide, so the only option is to work harder and sacrifice more to provide it. Check out the common theme at the heart of most of the stories of regret I have heard over trading relationships for money:

Who I am is not enough, so I had better work harder and longer to provide more.

Who I am as a father or mother is not enough. Who I am as a husband or wife is not enough. Who I am as son or daughter is not enough. I had better work more than one person should work so that I can provide more than what I really can. Maybe that will make me enough.

If you have struggled with trading relationships for money, I'm guessing that like most people, you are a good person with a loving heart who is doing her best to provide for the people she loves. I'm guessing that there is a part of you that believes you are not enough, which makes it easier to fall prey to the lure of more and the lie of being irreplaceable. But, because you are a good person with a loving heart, it can also make it easier for you to turn things around.

This was Liu Yang's story. He was one of my clients who was trading relationships for money. He had a beautiful young son and daughter that he almost never spent time with. He would get up each morning and go to work before his children woke up and arrive home each night after they went to bed. He worked eighty or ninety hours every week. When I pressed him on why he was working such long hours, he told me he had no choice.

This was his rationale: he had to work that many hours because he needed to get noticed. He needed to make a name for himself in the company. If he could do that, then he could get a certain promotion by the time his kids were out of elementary school. If that happened, he was almost sure he could reach a particular level in the company before his oldest child graduated from high school.

"And if that happens," he said in conclusion, "then I will be able to afford to pay for my children's college education."

I waited a moment and then asked the question.

"So, what happens if you don't work all those hours and you can't put your children through college?"

He looked at me like I had two heads. It was pretty funny, actually.

We talked more and it became clear that, to Liu Yang, if he didn't pay for his kids' college he would be a complete failure as a father.

So I pressed him some more.

"Liu Yang, imagine that you go home tonight, sit your son and daughter on the couch, and have this heart-to-heart conversation with them."

"Kids, I'm going to give you the choice of the life you want to have. You have two options. Option number one: I will not know you. I will not see you. I will be present on the weekends ,but I will be exhausted. Your mother and I will slowly drift apart because I won't be able to invest any time with her either, so you won't have any model for what real love and intimacy look like. I won't be able to help you learn how to ride a bike or play chess or shoot free throws. But here's the good news: when you are eighteen years old you will have four years of college, absolutely free."

"Here's option number two: I will be deeply imbedded in your life. I will constantly be there to remind you that you are strong and kind and beautiful. I will help frame your identity. I will play a critical role in everything that is important to you from now until you go to college. We will create countless precious memories together that belong only to us. Whenever you have a problem, I will be the safest person to turn to for help. Not only that, but I will do the same thing for your mother. She will be the number one priority in my life, and you both will know what it looks like for two people to be deeply in love and devoted to one another.

But here's the bad news: you can still go to college, but you'll have to get student loans."

I let the choices sit there for a moment, then I asked: "Which option do you think they will choose?"

He thought for a moment, and then he answered the same way every man and woman I've asked has answered.

"They would choose the second option," he said.

"So then why are you picking the one you know in your heart they don't want?"

I already knew the answer to that question. He was picking the option they didn't want because in his heart, Liu Yang struggled to believe the same thing that you and I struggle to believe: that who we are is enough, that it's enough for the people that we love to just have the normal, human-sized, non-superhero us who cannot provide the world on a silver platter.

And yet, he couldn't deny that he was choosing the option his children didn't want. So Liu Yang, because he was a good man with a loving heart, promised himself he would be deeply embedded in his children's life. He and his wife and his two kids had some important conversations and created their Lifestyle Cap.

And here was the surprising thing to Liu Yang. Because he was working a normal schedule, he wasn't exhausted all the time and he began to really love his work again. The quality and efficiency of his work rose steadily. Eventually, he did get noticed. He didn't rise as fast as he had planned, but he eventually rose further than even he had dreamed possible. And, yes, his children needed student loans to help get through college, but they are both doing well in life.

And the best part is they have a great relationship with their father, who at one point was the man who was never there, but learned to become the man who would never trade relationships for money.

CHAPTER 3

Don't Miss Opportunities to Be Generous

We don't understand how much value we get when we positively impact the lives of other human beings. Take, for example, the story of Tiffany.

Tiffany had never known anything but poverty. When she was three years old, she was sent to live with her aunt because her mother, who struggled with a drug addiction, had been evicted from their apartment and was now homeless. A year later, she was sent to live with a second aunt, because the first aunt just couldn't afford to have an extra child in the home. Over the next ten-plus years, Tiffany bounced around from one relative to another in three different states. At sixteen, she dropped out of school. At nineteen, she became pregnant. At twenty, she gave birth to a beautiful baby girl whom she named Taylor.

Like most of us, Tiffany was not prepared for how much love she would experience at the birth of a child. Taylor became Tiffany's whole world, and she was determined that Taylor would escape the cycle of poverty that she had lived in her whole life.

Fortunately for Tiffany, a local church offered a program that was exactly what she needed. Through course work and one-on-one mentoring, she gained a wide variety of job and interpersonal skills that she needed to lay a new foundation for her life. She worked hard to apply everything she was learning, and at twenty-seven years old she was completely off of government assistance, the first person in her entire extended family to accomplish this feat in at least three generations. She was proud of this accomplishment. More than this, she was hopeful about what kind of start she was giving to Taylor.

Then it happened.

It almost always happens in these stories.

Tiffany was offered a new job with a non-profit agency that provided rehabilitation services for drug addicts. Remembering her mother's struggles with drugs and the dramatic impact they had on her own life, this wasn't just a job for Tiffany, it was a calling. She found a house that she could rent near the new job, and she fell in love with it. She was thrilled with the idea of Taylor living in a real house with a real yard. Besides, it was so close to the new job. It must be fate. The problem was Tiffany could only afford to rent the house as long as nothing ever went wrong. So, for all the right reasons, she made the wrong decision. She decided to rent the house. Then something went wrong.

It was four months into the new job and new life, and Tiffany and Taylor had just come back from a week of vacation to discover that one of them had left the restroom faucet running. Not horrible, she thought — until she received the water bill for $1500. There was no way she could pay it off in time. Late fees were added to what she owed. She got behind on her rent trying to pay off the water bill, so late fees were added to her rent. She was in a downward spiral that she couldn't stop.

Two months later, her landlord evicted her. She was homeless in the middle of winter. Taylor had to go and stay with Tiffany's sister the next state over just to keep out of the cold. There was a $3700 judgment against her, which meant that her wages would be garnished to pay what she owed the landlord and the water company. She knew no one would rent her a new apartment with the judgment against her, and she couldn't afford one anyway. She was trapped. She would have to go back on government assistance. She was worried that Child Protective Services would step in and take Taylor away from her because she was going to be homeless. It was like she was living her mother's life all over again.

There are two things that I have seen to be true with people who are striving to break the cycle of poverty. The first is they have no margin for error. The second is they are going to make errors. We all make mistakes, but some of us have enough resources to absorb our mistakes without the consequences becoming cata-strophic. Tiffany couldn't absorb her mistakes. Seven years of hard work, and the cycle of poverty was start-ing all over again, and she knew this time it was Taylor's turn to ride.

And that's how the story would have continued, if it weren't for the generosity of one couple who had been mentors to Tiffany. They had seen how hard she had worked, and they knew that she would learn from this mistake and continue to grow. So they paid the $3700 judgment. That meant no wages were ever garnished from her check. It meant she was able to get a new apartment, this time one she could really afford, and Taylor only spent two weeks away from her mother, instead of the rest of her childhood. It meant Tiffany never went back on government assistance and now, four years later, continues to provide for herself and her daughter.

And here's what I want you to think about: how much value would it have added to your life if you were the person who was able to step in the gap for Tiffany and her daughter. How would it feel at Christmas when you knew that Tiffany and Taylor would be spending it together instead of in different states, and you had a hand in it? What would it be like for you to some-day watch Tiffany swell with pride as she watches Taylor graduate from high school and head off to college, knowing you played a role in making that happen?

We don't understand how much value we get when we positively impact the lives of other human beings. I believe that you will never feel more human, more alive, and more fulfilled than when you are being generous in a way that makes an impact on others.

You might think that in a book on finances that generosity would be the last chapter, not chapter three. For a lot of people, generosity is an afterthought. After you've built your fortune, after you have achieved all of your goals in life, after you've done everything you've wanted to do and have more money than you know what to do with, at that point it's time to think about being generous. But this isn't a book just about accumulating wealth. It's a book about accumulating wealth without accumulating regret. It's a book about how to live life fully while you are accumulating wealth. And here is one truth I run into again and again:

I've never met an unhappy generous person.

Never. The people I've met who are generous are the happiest people I know. It's like they have learned the secret of squeezing every last drop of joy out of life. And so, I want to challenge you to make the decision right now, even before we get into the nuts and bolts of creating a sound financial plan, to make generosity a part of your lifestyle.

Hard-Wired to Be Generous

I believe we are hard-wired to be generous. That is why we feel so alive and so human when we are generous. That is why when we watch A Christmas Carol, something in our heart leaps when Scrooge becomes the generous benefactor to all the people he had been ignoring or detesting. This hard-wiring towards giving is apparent even when we are very young. It never ceases to amaze and delight me that on Christmas morning, my kids' favorite moment is when they give me a present.

"Dad, can you open my present now?" one of them will say, and when I agree, they dash to the tree to get it and dash back to give it to me. Then, as I unwrap it, they bounce up and down as if they are about to come out of their skin, eager to see the look on my face when I see the pair of gloves they picked out for me. And after I open the present, they invariably will want to tell me the story of when they bought the present or why they picked that particular color. It really is one of the most beautiful moments of the entire year. Generosity is not just about charity. Generosity is about having an opportunity to use your resources to positively impact someone else's life. Opportunities are all around us, and when we see those opportunities, I believe that generosity is our first impulse.

Imagine, for example, that you're driving down the street and you see a very anxious mom with three young kids stranded on the side of the road with a flat tire. Isn't there a tug in your heart that says, "I wish I could help her," or "I wonder if they're going to be okay"? That's because generosity is your first impulse. Other thoughts might follow. Often, we dismiss that first impulse and tell ourselves, "If I stop and help I'll be late," or, "She's probably fine."

Why? Why do we have that first impulse to help followed by all the reasons why it's not practical or necessary?

Imagine you're at the gas station and across the pump from you, a young couple with three young kids pull up. You can tell by the way the car is rattling and sputtering that this is a family that is just scraping by. You think, "How easy would it be to swing around and swipe my card and pay for their gas? That might be 30 bucks they could spend on clothes for the kids, or groceries, or doing something fun." It would be so simple. Almost anyone could do it. But then you don't. Our first tug is to be generous, but then we talk ourselves out of it.

I wouldn't be surprised if these examples triggered in your mind a recent opportunity that came your way that sounds even more life-giving to you — and that you talked yourself out of. And whether it involved helping close friends, family, or complete strangers, whether it involved people in your city or people half a world away, whether it involved spending a few dollars or a few thousand dollars, something in your heart leapt when you thought, "I can make a difference here."

Let's be very clear about this so that we are talking about the same thing. With true generosity, there is always that sense of your heart coming alive. We have all experienced what it is like to get a phone call from a charity that we are not passionate about. We have all experienced what it is like when someone who is not taking responsibility for their lives wants us to give them money to solve the latest problem they have gotten themselves into. We don't feel any satisfaction in giving; we feel either dread or anger. When we do give in these situations, it is not to positively impact lives; it is usually to avoid conflict or guilt, and we end up feeling used. With true generosity, there is always the sense that we are freely choosing to give because there is a specific impact we want to make in the lives of others. This desire to make an impact is worth paying close attention to.

Which brings up a question: If it's true that we are hard-wired to be generous, and if it's true that we never feel more alive and more human than when we are being generous in a way that impacts other people, then why does it seem like such a challenge for us to live a generous lifestyle? Why do we keep talking ourselves out of these impulses?

Here's why.

Imagine you are in your kitchen cooking your favorite meal, when all of a sudden, everything goes dead. The lights go out, the blender stops working, and the electric stove won't heat. This sudden thrust back into the Stone Age doesn't mean that your house is no longer wired for electricity. More than likely, it means that a circuit breaker has tripped and is preventing the flow of electricity from reaching the kitchen. It also means that if you want the power to start flowing again, you have to find the right circuit breaker and click it back to the On position.

Generosity Circuit Breakers

I've noticed that there are three circuit breakers that, when tripped, will stop the natural flow of generosity in your life. Your heart will feel a kind of deadness until you find the right circuit breaker and click it back onto the right position.

The first circuit breaker is the *Fortunate/Self-Made* breaker. I've noticed that I can have two clients who have very similar successes in life: They have each climbed to the same point on the corporate ladder; they each have the same amount of money saved, the same big house, and the same fancy car. I can talk to one and she will talk about how fortunate she is, how many lucky breaks she has had along the way, and how blessed she is to have the natural talents and abilities that she possesses. I talk to the second client and she will talk about how she is a self-made woman, and how she has earned and deserves everything she has achieved in life.

Here is what I always find. The person who believes they have been fortunate is always much more generous and much more happy with life than the person who thinks they did it all by themselves. Don't get me wrong: the people who feel fortunate know they are smart and talented and that they have worked hard to get where they are in life. But they also know that there are a lot of other people who are just as smart and talented who have worked just as hard, but didn't have the same breaks or opportunities.

"I put in the work," I will often hear them say, "but I've got to be hones — I was also in the right place at the right time."

Maybe you are thinking, "I *would* feel fortunate too, but I haven't got the breaks that other people have had in life!" You might be right about that, but this leads to the second breaker.

The second circuit breaker is the *Grateful/Entitled* breaker, and I discovered it from a career of working with people from every spot on the economic continuum, from the very poor in developing nations, to the very rich in America, and here is what I can tell you with absolute certainty. No matter how much money and possessions you have, I know many people who have *much less* than you do who feel grateful for what they have. These grateful people tend to be very generous, and they thoroughly enjoy the life that they have. I also know many people who have *much more* than you do who feel like they are getting a raw deal in life and believe that they are entitled to more. These people are not able to enjoy what they do have, and believe that happiness will come in the future when they finally have everything that life owes them. This group has an extremely hard time being generous — unless there is a tax write-off. Let's be honest: that's not generosity. That's selfishness in disguise.

In other words, I have seen absolutely no correlation between how much you have and how happy you are, but I have seen a very strong correlation between how grateful you are for what you have and how happy you are. The gratitude always comes before the happiness; the entitlement always comes before the unhappiness.

And that leads us to the third circuit breaker, which is the Abundance/Scarcity breaker. If you have an abundance mentality, you believe that there are enough resources for everyone. You believe you have more than you need and will continue to have more than you need tomorrow. If you have a scarcity mentality, you believe there are not enough resources to go around, and that we are all in competition for those resources. Those with an abundance mentality have a sense that they are thriving, while those with a scarcity mentality always feel like they are in survival mode. Because of this, those with a scarcity mentality have a hard time enjoying what they have, let alone being generous with what they have.

You might assume that the more someone has, the more they are likely to have an abundance mentality. But that's not the case. Again, I've worked with people at every spot on the economic continuum, and at every spot, I've met people who have an abundance mentality and people who have a scarcity mentality. How much you have does not create an abundance mentality or a scarcity mentality, but which outlook you have does impact how much you are enjoying what you have.

Here is what I've learned: When I meet someone who struggles with generosity, it doesn't mean that they are a selfish person. It just means that one or more of these circuit breakers has been tripped and needs to be reset. Once we reset our circuit breakers, we are not only able to consistently practice generosity towards others, but we are amazed at how much more energy and joy we feel towards others and towards the life that we have.

So let's talk about how we reset those circuits and keep them in the right position.

The Abundance Fund

Let's start with a very concrete, practical question: How much money could you intentionally put towards being generous each month and still meet all of your current financial obligations while saving enough for your future? If you are like most people, the honest answer is "I have no idea." And that is the crux of the problem. If you don't have a sound financial plan that you trust, any answer to this question is just a guess. And here is what I've noticed: when we guess, we assume the worst. When we guess, we err on the side of scarcity. That's just a part of human nature. When we are uncertain, we become very cautious and hesitant. I've met with new clients who really have been doing a great job with their finances — even saving like crazy — but because they didn't have a plan that they trusted, it still felt like they were living paycheck to paycheck. They were doing well, but they were still in survival mode. Can you hear those circuit breakers tripping?

On the other hand, when we have a sound plan that we trust, we know what reality is. We know how much we can give without being irresponsible, and that gives us the confidence to give freely. One of the things I love most about my job is that I am in the business of giving people the confidence to be generous.

"This year. you could give away $40,000 and you wouldn't miss it," I recently told a couple who are clients of mine. As we reviewed their plan and how things had been progressing, they realized that I was right. They didn't leave that meeting hoping that they could be generous; they left the meeting with their eyes wide open, looking for every opportunity that came their way. That's the value of knowing your current reality, and it only happens when you have a financial plan.

Part of your plan must include having what I call an Abundance Fund. The Abundance Fund is your primary defense against those three circuit breakers getting tripped into the wrong position, so let me define it for you.

The Abundance Fund is money that you set aside to be ready when the opportunity to be generous comes your way.

The Abundance Fund is a product of the Lifestyle Cap that we talked about in the last chapter. Once you've set your lifestyle cap, everything that comes in that is over and above that number goes to charities that you want to support on a regular basis and into the Abundance Fund.

The Abundance Fund is not a theoretical account in a budget. It is an actual separate bank account that you create, and you only take money out of that account when you have an opportunity to be generous. Remember the examples of opportunities we talked about earlier in the chapter? What difference would it make if, when you came across the young mother with a flat tire or the young, struggling couple at the gas station, you already had the money to help set aside in a separate account?

Let me give you the answer because I've seen it in action: It would make all the difference in the world. You would start consistently acting on those generous impulses and enjoy each one. You would experience a different level of meaning and satisfaction because of the impact you would be making on the lives of others. Generosity would become more than an idea; it would become a part of your lifestyle. It would become part of the culture of your family.

One of the great things about having an abundance fund in my family is that our kids know that it is there and it gives them opportunities to practice being generous. One year, one of my sons was going to summer camp, and he knew that the mother of one of his closest friends was going through some pretty tough cancer treatment. It was a hard season for that whole family. My son asked if we could use part of the abundance fund to pay for his friend to come to camp with him.

"What a great idea," I said. "Of course we can!"

When your kids know that you have a fund set aside to be generous, they look for ways to make an impact.

That's a practice that will help keep their circuit breakers in the right position throughout their lives.

I don't know if you can afford to put five dollars, fifty dollars, or five hundred dollars in your Abundance Fund each month. You can figure out the details as you get into the nuts and bolts of your financial plan. The important thing is that you realize right now how important it is to your happiness to make an impact on the lives of others, and to put yourself in the position to do that on a regular basis.

Resetting Your Generosity Circuit Breakers

The Lifestyle Cap and the Abundance Fund are two powerful instruments that will not only switch your generosity circuit breakers back to the On position. Their presence in your financial plan will ensure that each of these breakers stay in the On position.

As we emphasized in the last chapter, the Lifestyle Cap will keep you anchored to the people who are most important to you, which will do more than anything else to help you experience abundance. But it will do more than that. It will help you to define where your happiness comes from. It will protect you from having to keep up with the Joneses, or fall prey to the latest advertising blitz telling you that you are falling behind and that you absolutely need more. By determining that you have all you need right now to be happy, you have positioned yourself to have an abundance view of life. The Lifestyle Cap resets your abundance circuit breaker.

The Abundance Fund, on the other hand, locks the abundance circuit breaker in the On position. It doesn't matter if you have $50 or $5,000 in your abundance fund; its very presence is concrete, irrefutable proof that you have more than you need. The joy you experience each time you use your Abundance Fund to make a difference will reinforce the mindset of abundance. Having a profound impact in the lives of others will help you experience abundance much more than the accumulation of things.

The Abundance Fund will also keep the Fortunate/Self-Made breaker in the On position. One of the things that keeps us stuck in the Self-Made view is the idea that, "That's my money, I earned it all by myself. How dare someone ask for it?" When we set up an abundance fund, we do two things to combat this attitude. First, we have already decided, "That's not my money — that's money that I want to pay forward because of all the ways that I've been fortunate in my life." The second thing the abundance fund does to keep this circuit breaker switched On is constantly remind us how life really works. In the beginning of The Christmas Carol, Scrooge sees himself as a self-made man, but his trip with the Ghost of Christmas Past helps him see life really doesn't work that way. He realizes how much his first boss, Mr. Fezziwig, treated him like a son. He trained him, mentored him, and gave him opportunities that were essential to his later success. The abundance fund will remind you to reflect on all of the things that have contributed to your current success that you had nothing to do with. You weren't born in the middle ages during a plague. You weren't born in a third world country where you have to walk three miles to the nearest source of water. You have certain inherent traits towards intelligence or creativity or networking that you didn't create — they have been a part of who you are since you were a child. These things are just the backdrop of your life, and they have as much or more to do with your success than the decisions you made or the work that you've done. Add to this backdrop all of the people who have had direct impact on your success — teachers, counselors, co-workers, family and friends — and it's easy to remember how fortunate you have been.

This reflection on all the ways that you've been fortunate creates an upward spiral that keeps your circuit breaker in the On position. As with Scrooge, you immediately want to start giving others the same kind of fortunate opportunities you realize have come your way. Like Scrooge, you make another discovery: people start responding to you differently. People who have a fortunate view of life are so much more attractive, human, and approachable than people who have a self-made perspective.

Can you see how this focus on abundance and having been fortunate can keep the grateful/entitled circuit breaker in the right position? One of the common fears I hear from people is that if they use the abundance fund to help people, they will create entitled, dependent relationships. Won't people just keep coming back for more? I have found that the opposite is true. When you give, you have an opportunity to sit down and explain the idea of the abundance fund to someone and say, "Here's why I'm doing this." It changes the paradigm of giving.

I always explain that this is not about me being the hero. This is about recognizing how fortunate I've been and how grateful I am, and wanting to pass that experience on to others. My experience has been that this approach generates gratitude in others rather than entitlement, and it creates a desire in them to do the same thing in others' lives.

Missed Opportunities

I had a client who was in his eighties and was really struggling with what he was going to do with his ten million dollars. He was afraid that if he gave it to his children before he died, they would be reckless and irresponsible and waste the fortune he had built.

"Fred, you know you're going to die," I said, trying to be as gentle as possible but still wanting to help him to see reality. "So your kids are going to get this money. So what's going to be different after you're dead? Will they be any more responsible?"

"No, they'll still waste it," he said gruffly.

"So do you want to disinherit them? Do you want to give it all to charity?"

"No, I want the kids to get it."

"So, the kids are going to get the money. That's not in question. You have two choices to make. Do you want to give them an opportunity to be exposed to this extra that they've never had before while you're still alive? Do you want to give it to them in little bits and starts so they can practice handling the money? Or do you want them to go from living in the desert to having this ocean dumped on them?"

I could tell he was seeing my point, so I continued. "Here's the second question. Do you want to watch them enjoy it? Do you want to watch them experience your generosity? Do you want to feel the connection that you can have with your kids when you are making an impact on their lives?

"Or," I continued, "Do you want them to say, 'Thank goodness he died because I finally have what I need.'?

Fred started taking small steps in being generous with his children and, just like Scrooge in A Christmas Carol, he was surprised at how the relationships opened up. His children became more honest with him because he was more involved in their lives. He had always been withdrawn, and his kids were very aware that he had money because he would lord it over them. They wouldn't talk to him about their struggles, because they knew he would just shame them and talk about how he was a self-made man. They knew that any vulnerability would result in feeling stupid. But things changed when he started being generous.

He gave one of his kids $10,000, just as a practice run. When he later asked him what he did with it, his son said that he used it to pay off some credit card debt. His son was honest about some bad financial choices he had made, and he talked about the difference it made in his life and marriage to get some of that weight off of his shoulders. It was obvious that he deeply appreciated his father's generosity. Something in Fred's heart melted a little bit in that conversation and he asked how much it would take to get the couple completely caught up, which he immediately gave to his son. The couple got caught up financially and began to experience margin, which was a life-changer, and Fred was there to experience their gratitude.

And in response to his generosity, his children were finally able to see their dad as a resource. They asked his advice in financial matters; they felt safe to open up about mistakes they had made, which, oddly enough, turned out to be very similar to mistakes he had made when he was their age. They sought his guidance in career decisions. They began to share parts of their lives with him that had nothing to do with money.

As so often is the case, once Fred's generosity switches got turned on, he even began to look outside his family for opportunities to be generous because he saw the value in it outside his family as well.

Fred died five years later, and the relationship he had with his children still wasn't as close as he would have liked. I know he felt a deep regret for all the wasted years that had gone before. But the relationships were closer than they had been for a long time, and his kids were left with memories of a father who was genuinely trying to make a difference in their lives.

Sometimes, as in the case with Fred, there is a fear behind the lack of generosity: If I give it to them, it's going to make them lazy; if I give it to them, they're going to want more; if I give it to them I will make them dependent. While these are legitimate concerns and need to be considered, the tragedy is when these fears prevent us from expressing any generosity towards our family and friends.

I've known people who are just about to retire and have built up their own fortune and then receive a large inheritance. And the response is "Whatever, Dad. I don't need it now." They could have used a fraction of it twenty years ago when they were working two jobs to pay off the medical bills, or when they were trying to adopt a child but couldn't afford it. There were moments when they could have used a little leg up to get through a crisis. Just a little help at critical moments in life would have meant much more than millions after Mom and Dad are gone. How sad is it when someone leaves behind the sum total of their life savings and it only serves to underscore the lack of connection they had with the people who mattered most to them?

I want something better for you, and thankfully, it's never too late make a difference.

Redeeming Missed Opportunities

Irene is one of my favorite people in the whole world. She is 91-years old and full of life. Whenever I visit her in the nursing home, she grabs my arm and — all five-foot-two of her — walks me to the cafeteria to have our meeting. Instantly, because everyone knows her, they begin asking who this nice young man is.

"Oh, he's my lover," she claims impishly, and it always makes me howl with laughter.

Irene has always been a grateful person, but for whatever reason, she never practiced generosity. So in one of our meetings years ago, I brought up the subject.

"Irene, you are not going to outlive all this money. So what do you want to be remembered for after you are gone?"

"I'm really passionate about the public library," she said, not even needing a moment to consider. "They want to build a new computer lab with new equipment."

"Write the check," I said.

So Irene wrote the check, and she liked it. She liked the way it felt knowing she was making a difference. She started writing more checks. She started giving money away like crazy. In a six-week period, she gave away $60,000.

"Am I giving too much money away?" she asked me. I said, "Go! Keep going!" I felt like a track coach standing on the sideline and cheering a newly discovered superstar. One of my favorite moments was the day the new computer lab opened at the public library and it had her name on it.

The next time I met with her, I had good news and bad news. "The good news," I said, "is that you gave away almost $100,000 this year. The bad news is it wasn't enough. Your portfolio made $250,000. You're getting behind!"

So she kept writing checks. One day, she called me out of the blue to say, "I'm so glad I'm doing this. This is the most fun I've ever had!"

I don't want you to wait until you're 91 to have the most fun you've ever had. I want that experience to be a thread that runs through every season of your life. You are hard-wired to be generous. You are hard-wired to experience joy when you make a profound impact in other people's lives. When we see Ebenezer Scrooge transform from the stingy, bitter man to the generous, joyful man in one night, we absolutely believe it. In one night, he becomes the best version of Ebenezer Scrooge, because the circuit breakers are switched and his natural impulse towards generosity is able to flow. With the security that comes from having a financial plan that includes an Abundance Fund, you can make sure you are living the version of your life that you really want to live.

CHAPTER 4

Create and Protect Margin

One of the most destructive financial regrets we can experience is living with too much financial stress for too long, and allowing that stress to build, to preoccupy our attention, and to steal our enjoyment of much of the good things in our lives.

Stress itself is not a bad thing. I'm a runner, and when I run, I am purposely putting extra stress on my cardiovascular system. When I do that, an amazing thing happens. Without even having to think about it, my body flexes to handle the extra stress. My heart rate and blood pressure increase, my blood vessels expand to accommodate extra blood flow, and more oxygen is delivered to the muscles that are doing the extra work. When I stop running, everything flexes back to my normal resting state. I call the body's ability to go into an extra gear to handle extra stress margin.

Margin is a great thing, because extra stress is a normal part of life. Imagine you are walking along and realize you have to climb three flights of stairs to get to where you want to go. If you have margin, that's no problem. Your body flexes to absorb the extra stress as you climb the stairs. But if your heart is already beating at maximum capacity, and if your blood vessels have already expanded to their limit, then you have a problem. If that's the case, you're probably going to have a heart attack half-way up!

Since moments of extra stress are a normal part of life, it's a good idea to engage in regular, disciplined aerobic exercise because this increases the amount of margin that you have available.

Financial stress is also a normal part of life. Cars break down, basements get flooded, unexpected medical bills pop up — these are all normal parts of life. And, just like encountering the extra three flights of stairs, if we have margin, we can flex and accommodate the extra stress and continue on our way. If we are already maxed out financially, these normal stresses can become catastrophic. Even waiting for the catastrophe causes our heart rate to elevate and our palms to sweat. It's an ever-present state of anxiety.

Financial margin is having the confidence and peace of mind that you can handle the unexpected stresses that life will throw at you. The more financial margin we have, the more we have beyond what is actually necessary, the better equipped we are to handle financial stress. And just like aerobic exercise, there are regular disciplines that we can practice that increase our financial margin.

Now, I'm guessing that you are tracking with me to this point, but you're also a little nervous that I'm going to drop the B-bomb on you: Budget. After all the typical, traditional answer to not having enough margin is to create a budget. If you just create a budget and categorize your spending, you'll be fine. But my guess is that you've already tried a budget and it didn't work. My guess is that you have absolutely no faith in budgets. And believe it or not, I think there are really good reasons why you think that way.

Welcome to Budget Prison. We Hope You Enjoy Your Stay.

What is the first thing that comes to mind when you hear the word *budget?* My guess is that it is not positive. My guess is that when someone says *budget,* you do not picture yourself on a tropical beach drinking margaritas. I imagine that when someone says *budget,* you instead picture yourself in a jail cell eating spam and ramen noodles. And I'm guessing that a part of you believes you have to convince yourself to stay in that prison cell and deny yourself all enjoyment for the next twenty-five years so that you can retire with a little bit of money to enjoy the remaining years of your life.

Who wants that?

If you are married, there is a bigger problem with budget prison. I've noticed that in most relationships, there is a person that I call Go and a person that I call Whoa. The attitude of Go is, *Who cares about consequences? Let's just go have fun right now.* The attitude of Whoa is, *Slow down. Let's think about this. This probably isn't such a good idea.* I bet it only took you about six seconds to decide who is Go and who is Whoa in your relationship. So you know what happens when you put Go and Whoa in budget prison? Go becomes the prisoner and Whoa becomes the warden. Go feels overly restricted and looks for every chance to break free, while

Whoa sees the budget as the perfect tool to keep Go in check. Tension and resentment build between Go and Whoa. The more Go wants to spend, the more Whoa feels the need to clamp down. The more Whoa clamps down, the more Go wants to spend. The budget doesn't become a tool to help build wealth and enjoy life; it becomes a constant power struggle.

Now, Go and Whoa didn't fall in love and commit to a relationship so that one of them could be a prisoner and one of them could be the jailer, yet every time a money conversation comes up, that is exactly what it feels like. Pretty soon, they give up even mentioning the budget and let it die a quiet death, just to bring some peace back to the relationship.

Does any of this sound familiar? Here's the bigger problem that I see. When people hear that creating a budget is the key to financial success but they experience the budget as a horrible, life-stealing prison, the conclusion they usually draw is, *I guess I will just struggle along financially because I obviously don't have what it takes to build wealth.* They give up. Perhaps at some point you gave up. I want to convince you that you do have what it takes to build wealth, and you can start that journey today.

Budgets and Regret

Let's talk about the real problem. The reason that most people hate budgets is because budgets are created at the wrong time, in the wrong way, and for the wrong reason. If that's not enough to guarantee failure, I don't know what is. Here's an example of what happens every day in a relationship somewhere. Go really wants to buy a new car. In fact, Go has already emotionally committed to buying the new car. But Go needs to prove to himself and to Whoa that buying a new car is financially responsible. So what does Go do? He creates a budget, of course.

Go knows that the monthly payment on the new car is going to be $349 month. He also knows how much he and Whoa bring in each month, so he knows how much he has to work with. He then totals up all the fixed expenses each month to see what is left over. And here is where Go gets creative.

"Hmm," he says to himself, "if each month, we spend only x amount on groceries, and x amount on entertainment, and x amount on clothes, and x amount on doctors' visits, then look! We have just enough to afford the car payment."

Now, where does the x amount in each category come from? Go simply pulls the numbers from thin air. Go has already decided that he is going to make the numbers fit. In fact, Go has absolutely no idea how much is spent each month on groceries or if x amount means a drastic reduction or a huge increase. But, Go has budget. And a budget is the key to financial responsibility.

With this statistical proof in hand, Go approaches Whoa. Whoa has a couple different reactions. First of all, Whoa has been asking for a budget for years, so this sounds very promising. It sounds like a step in the right direction. Secondly, although some of the categories seem a little austere, that's okay because, to be honest, Whoa kind of likes austerity. It feels sober. It feels like a challenge that Go and Whoa are going to tackle togeth-er, which is really what Whoa has wanted all along — to be a team when it comes to finances. So Whoa signs off on the deal, they get the new car, and they've added $349 to their monthly expenses.

Then reality sets in. The x amount set aside for gro-ceries is a 30% reduction in what they've usually spent, which means a drastic change in their daily menu. The x amount set aside for entertainment means going out only once a month rather than one or two times a week, which is what they have been doing. The x amount on clothes is actually more than they need, but that's more than swallowed up by the extra doctors' visits they've needed to make. And, by the way, Go forgot to put in several categories, so even that cup of coffee he loves to get on the way to the office is now enough to break the bank.

And here is why this is such a big problem:

Go and Whoa agreed on a budget that eliminated their margin.

But it's even worse. Go and Whoa didn't just elimi-nate their margin for this month. Since they got a loan to buy the car, they eliminated their margin for the next five years. But it's even worse than that. They eliminated their margin for the next five years for a purchase they will regret in five months! In five months the new car smell will be gone and the car will be worth less than what they owe on it. And sadly, it's even worse than that. Because Go and Whoa are now in Budget Prison, they get to take up the familiar roles of prisoner and warden. Let the tension begin. It doesn't take too long before Go starts to rebel against the tight budget. Whoa is surprised and disappointed that the budget hasn't created the united team she was hoping for and feels betrayed each time Go overspends on any category. In creating a budget, Go and Whoa did what they thought was right. They did what they always heard they should do. Somehow, it backfired on them. We can't even keep a simple budget, they think. How on earth are we ever going to save for retirement? Maybe you've been there before and thought the same thing.

But just like Go and Whoa buying a car, we usually create budgets at the wrong time, for the wrong reason, in the wrong way, and with the wrong results. It's really easy to get caught up in this process. We are constantly bombarded by advertisements. And these are not naïve attempts to get our money, but sophisticated messages based on in-depth research into human psychology and decision making. Let's look back at the details of this situation:

- When: We create budgets when we have become convinced that we need something that we really don't need.

- Why: We create budgets to justify to ourselves and others that we can buy something we don't need.

- How: We Create budgets by picking imaginary numbers out of thin air.

- Result: Our financial margin disappears.

Then we get to spend five years in Budget Prison because we bought something we're over in five months, and we doom ourselves to constant power struggles with the person who is most important to us.

No wonder you hate budgets. To be honest, I don't like them very much either. I'd rather talk about having a Spending Plan.

Budget Prison vs. Spending Plan

Let's get the semantics out of the way first. I don't like the connotations of the word budget. When you hear the word budget, you automatically think restriction, or tightening the belt, or reducing your life to fit into this little box. I like the words Spending Plan. A Spending Plan is an agreement that we are going to spend our money. We'll spend some of it on clothes, some of it date night, some of it on creating margin, some of it on being generous, and some of it when we retire, but we are going to spend it. A budget focuses on not spending money. A Spending Plan says, "We are going to go on vacation and spend this much money and we are not going to feel guilty about it." A budget says, "If we skip vacation this year, we can come in under budget. Won't that be great?"

There are three basic steps to creating a Spending Plan:

- Define your current reality.
- Define what you want your reality to be.
- Protect new margin rather than spending it.

Take the Hank and Tammy Schmidt, for example. When I met them, they had no margin and were living week-to-week, under constant financial stress.

I started asking them some basic questions, like "How much do you spend on groceries?"

The answer I got was typical: "We could probably get by spending $250 on groceries."

"That's not what I asked," I said. "What do you spend?" Like most people, they had no idea. Unlike most budgets, Spending Plans are not created by pulling numbers out of thin air. The first step in creating a Spending Plan is simply having a spending journal so you get a clear grasp of your current reality. You can use websites, apps, software, or even good old paper and pen, but you need to start the process by figuring out exactly how much you spend in each area. That way, any decisions you make on how to proceed will be based on reality rather than wishful thinking.

As Hank and Tammy kept their spending journal, they got a clear understanding of how they spent their money each month and they were able to identify all the things that they thought were wasteful.

Here's another thing that happened as Hank and Tammy reviewed their spending journal. They saw that the weekend trips that they took every two or three months cost about $350 each trip. As they talked about eliminating that expense, they realized that these adventures were just too important. They always came back energized and closer to one another. They decided to keep that as part of their spending plan, which turned out to be a great decision. Not only did they get excited about planning the next trip, their motivation to create and protect their margin increased, because they knew that having margin would ensure that they could keep taking these trips together.

That's the second part of creating a Spending Plan — defining what you want your reality to look like. What is worth spending your money on? This does some pretty important things for you.

First, it helps you avoid impulsive spending. Remember those ads? It's a lot harder for them to work when you have a Spending Plan. It's hard to say *No* in a vacuum. When you haven't figured out where your happiness comes from and what it's going to cost, it's much harder to say *No* when that new, big, shiny toy comes along and promises to make you feel successful and important. If you've already figured out what a great life looks like for you, it's much easier to say *No* because your Spending Plan defines your *Yes*. And when you know what is most important to say *Yes* to, it is much easier to say *No* to all the shiny new toys that have nothing to do with your happiness.

Secondly, having a Spending Plan helps Go and Whoa finally become a team that actually enjoys talking about finances. When you have created a Spending Plan, you've built in the Go parts because you've already decided that taking a vacation each year or having a date night every other week or having a movie fund are essentials that you will not give up. Go can relax and enjoy life because he or she knows that what makes their motor run and makes life worth living has already been accounted for. There is actually a plan to spend money in those areas. When Go goes to the movies, he doesn't have to feel guilty or worry about an argument later, because that is exactly what the movie money is there for. You've also built in the Whoa parts because you've already decided why you are spending your money in some ways and not in others, and how much money you're going to spend in each area. Whoa gets to experience the teamwork and the purposeful spending that is so critical to his or her happiness.

It also gives Go and Whoa a way to talk about financial decisions that builds the relationship instead of causing a meltdown. I have a client who is definitely a Go. He recently went home and told his wife he wanted to get third car.

"Why?" said his Whoa wife. It was a reasonable question, since they each already owned a really nice car, and there wasn't a third driver in the family. Was this a mid-life crisis? Was this going to be a knock-down, drag out money fight? No, because they had a Spending Plan. When this couple created their Lifestyle Cap, one of the things they both agreed on was that they wanted to help people escape poverty. They regularly used their Abundance Fund for this purpose.

"I have a problem," he answered. "When I go to meet with someone in section eight housing and I pull up in my BMW, they make a judgment. They think, This guy doesn't understand or, This guy's going to think I'm stupid and it creates barriers. From the beginning, they don't trust me. My car is helpful when meeting with business clients, but it's really hurting me in connecting with people that we want to help. I want to get a used Toyota that doesn't cause that barrier. And, when people need help because their car is in the shop, we can lend them one of ours since we will have three."

It was a five minute discussion. It fit their Spending Plan. It didn't threaten their margin. So the Whoa wife was very enthusiastic about saying yes.

The third part of creating a plan is to protect new margin rather than spending it. Just before I had met with the Schmidts for the first time, Tammy had received a $200 a month raise. Like most people, her first thought was, What can I spend this on? She went out and bought a new furniture set. Not an extravagant set, but the payments were going to be $210.00 a month for 12 months. So the impact of the raise was they were going to have ten dollars less margin each month.

They decided this had to change. So, when Hank got a $180 a month raise, instead of buying the new carpet they wanted, they put it all into creating margin. Things were starting to snowball. After a year, Tammy got another raise of $85 dollars a month and the furniture was paid off. That was $295 a month for margin. And, since they had been building margin for the past year, they were able to pay cash for the new carpet that they wanted.

One day, out of the blue, I got a call from Tammy. "The water heater quit on us," she said.

"That's not good news," I said. "No, it's not," she said, "but it's also not stressful. We have enough margin to get it replaced without having to worry about it."

Hank and Tammy were living with a very healthy resting heart rate. This happened because they got out of Budget Prison and created a Spending Plan. When you look at the two processes side by side, it's easy to see the difference.

- When: We create budgets when we have become convinced that we need something that we really don't need. We create Spending Plans when we are not feeling pressured or motivated to buy something.

- Why: We create budgets to justify to ourselves and others that we can buy something we don't need. We create Spending Plans to ensure that we are putting our money towards the things we value most in life.

- How: We create budgets by picking imaginary numbers out of thin air. We create Spending Plans by getting a clear picture of reality, making appropriate adjustments, and protecting any new margin that comes our way.

- Results: Budgets eliminate our financial margin and create financial anxiety. Spending Plans increase our margin and create financial confidence and peace of mind.

Debt and Margin

There is a lot of conversation in the financial world about good debt and bad debt, or even if there is ever such a thing as good debt. To me, the idea of good debt versus bad debt has everything to do with margin.

When you take on debt, you are always losing margin for the duration of the debt. That means you are always adding some amount of stress to your life. Is this the "forty minutes on the elliptical machine" kind of stress, the type that is going to make you stronger financially, or is it the "climbing three flights of stairs when you are already at maximum heart rate" kind of stress?

That depends on the answer to two questions. The first question: *Is the debt leveraged for me or against me?* All debt is essentially leverage: you are using someone else's money now, to buy what you want now; in return, you are forfeiting your future money to repay the loan. If you are buying something that will be worth more than what you paid for it, then the debt is leveraged in your favor. If you end up paying more than the value of the purchase, then the debt is leveraged against you.

The second question is: *Can I tolerate the amount of margin I'm losing for the duration of this loan?* Perhaps the easiest way to understand what these two questions means and how they help you evaluate debt is to apply them to the various kinds of debt that are available to us.

Home Loans and Margin

Let's apply the first question to a mortgage loan. *Is this debt leveraged for me or against me?* If the house you are buying will continue to increase in value over the life of the loan so that it will be worth more than what you paid for it, then you have the potential of gaining financial strength by adding that stress to your life. It could be the financial equivalent of forty minutes a day on the treadmill. The debt is leveraged in your favor. I used the word *potential* because we still need to answer the second question.

Can I tolerate the amount of margin I'm losing by taking on this loan? Think about how much margin is built into the human body. Experts tell us if we want to burn fat through aerobic exercise, we should stay at 60-70% of our maximum heart rate for no longer than 80 minutes. If we want to increase our aerobic conditioning, we need to be at 70-80% of our maximum heart rate for no more than 40 minutes. We can tolerate running with only 30-40% margin of our maximum heart rate for about 80 minutes if we want to burn fat. That means we still have 20-30% of our aerobic margin left. When it comes to taking on debt, we always need to know how much of our margin we are losing, and for how long.

Let's say you've done your research and determined that the loan is leveraged in your favor. Can you tolerate the amount of margin you are losing by taking on the loan? You need to determine what the mortgage payment will do to your Spending Plan. Will you still have money for your weekly date night? Will you still have enough for the yearly vacation that you decided was so important to you? Will you still be able to protect your Abundance Fund so that you are impacting other people's lives? Will you be able to pay the monthly mortgage without worrying about your other financial obligations? Will you be able to absorb unexpected and emergency expenses that will come your way without going into crisis mode? And, since we are talking about a home loan, will you still be able to do this not only next month or next year, but for the next 30 years?

You need to decide how much debt you can take on before you ever talk to the bank. Banks love to tell you that you can afford a $400,000 home, even though they know absolutely nothing about you. They have no idea what a mortgage on a

$400,000 home would do to your Spending Plan. Then you go shopping for a home in that price range, and you fall in love with what that buys you. If you are not careful, you will experience the very definition of house-poor. So much of your money will go into paying your mortgage that there is no money left to enjoy life. Not all mortgage debt is good debt, because if you take on too much debt, you are going to live the life of a pauper in order to live in a castle.

This is a critical thing to think through. If you decide to spend a hundred bucks on a new set of plates for your kitchen, that might affect your margin for that month, but going into debt impacts your margin for years, if not decades. It's imperative to know how much margin you are losing and what kind of stress that is going to create.

Here's another important rule of thumb that I have found helpful to keep you from selling off too much margin: never, ever take on debt today with the expectation that your margin will increase tomorrow. It can be tempting to think "I know it makes things really tight now, but after I get my raise, my margin will be fine" or "after the sale goes through, I will get my margin back." This is how people start to get upside-down and backwards with their finances. When deciding whether to take on debt, assume that your margin will not change. Debt that you take on today must be based on today's margin.

Student Loans

Are student loans leveraged for you? The answer is: it depends. You must remember that just like banks and car dealerships, colleges are heavily incentivized to get you to buy their product — in this case, credit hours. Colleges love to tell you that student loans are a good investment, and to support this they will cite studies that say that people who go to college make more money. This is a well-worded lie. People who go to college don't make any more money than people who don't. What the studies do show is that people who graduate from college make more money than those who don't go to college. If you take out student loans without a high degree of certainty that you are going to graduate and use the degree professionally, then there is a good chance this debt will be heavily leveraged against you. You will end up owing tens of thousands of dollars for something that has added nothing to your income.

What about the second question: Can you tolerate the amount of margin you will lose by taking on this loan? First, this is the only exception to my rule of thumb to never take on a loan based on what you think your margin will look like tomorrow. Student loans are by nature taken out with the expectation that you will have a much higher salary at the time the loan comes due.

But too many people assume they will have enough margin to pay back a loan when they graduate, and that can get you into real trouble. You will need to do some research to determine two things. First, you need to know what the average starting salary is for your chosen profession. Secondly, you will need to know how competitive the market for those jobs will be when you graduate. Not all student loans are created equal. In today's market, if you're going to school to become a computer engineer there's a pretty good chance you will be able to find a job. If you're going to school to become a sports journalist or film director, you're going to find much stiffer competition to get a job in your chosen profession. You can't count on getting a job that will result in the margin you need.

This is critical to understand, because student loans are so easy to get that it creates the impression that they must be a good investment. But just as student loans can open up future possibilities, they can also close down future possibilities. I was meeting with a young lady recently who had was under constant financial stress. She had almost a hundred thousand dollars in student loan debt from her marketing degree, but she was working part-time as an art instructor. She said she took that job because it made her come alive. I had to be honest and let her know that this was an option that was not open to her. She had to get a job in marketing just so she could make enough money to pay back her loan. She would never be able to build margin and get her finances back to normal as a part-time art instructor.

Car Loans and Margin

Is the debt leveraged for me or against me? Let's say you purchase a $20,000 car on a five-year loan at 5% interest. Over the next five years you will pay over $22,600 in principle and interest. Because the value of automobiles depreciates so quickly, car loans are always leveraged against you. Generally, they only have enough value to provide a down payment on the next car loan. When you sell off some of your margin for a car loan, the stress that is created is never the kind of stress that is going to make you stronger.

But is it the kind of stress that will do damage? That depends on the answer to the second question.

Can I tolerate the amount of margin I'm losing for the duration of this loan? Sometimes people just really want to have a new car. They want to have the new car smell and the latest gadgets. Getting a loan to have that experience is never going to help them financially, but it doesn't necessarily mean it's going to harm them either. Again, you have to look at the level of margin you will have after factoring in the loan payment and ask yourself what that will do to your Spending Plan. What is that going to do to your quality of life? Will you still have enough to respond to the emergencies that will inevitably pop up? If the loan takes away too much margin, it will end up doing real damage to you.

Again, never trust the car dealers to tell you how much debt you can afford. They love to say "based on your credit score and income, you can afford to buy this car." Then they have you sit in and fall in love with a car that will destroy your margin.

If you want to build financial strength, then staying away from car loans is your best move. When you drive a car that is completely paid off, you are buying back margin every month. And if you save that margin, then when you go to buy the next car, you just pay cash — and you still have your monthly margin. And the only way to do that is to drive a clunker for a while.

Credit Card Debt and Margin

Is the debt leveraged for me or against me? When I talk to someone that has a significant amount of credit card debt, I ask them, "what did you use this for? What did all this debt buy you?" They usually can't answer the question because they have no idea. It's a hodgepodge of purchases: groceries, random items from Target, video games, nights out, meals at restaurants — all of which are instantly worthless. You can't resell it. If you have $8,000 worth of credit card debt, then you've spent that entire $8,000 on stuff that has already been consumed, or that your only option is to give it away. And yet you're paying 18% interest on stuff that is already worth zero in value. It is the ultimate example of leverage working against you.

The financial industry's biggest win is to convince you that credit card debt is no big deal. After all, the minimum monthly payments are so small! Yes, for the rest of your life, while the principal keeps getting bigger and bigger. There is simply no way you can win with credit card debt.

Can I tolerate the amount of margin I'm losing for the duration of this loan? Here's the reality. Credit card debt is the dead giveaway that someone has sold all their margin. When someone is putting monthly expenses on a card they can't pay off in full each month, they are at a negative margin.

Negative margin. Think about that for a moment. Negative margin is like being at your maximum heart rate and always having climb stairs. That's why I always challenge people with major credit card debt to treat it as a scorched earth scenario: sell the house, sell the car, do whatever you have to do — you don't have the option to wait this out! At 18% interest with those kind of numbers, you can't recover. And when I say "major credit card debt" I mean any debt that keeps growing each month. If you don't have a realistic plan to pay down your credit card debt, do whatever it takes to get out of it.

I Can Pick 'em Out of a Crowd

The last time I got a physical, the doctor casually said "you must be a runner."

"That's right," I said, "how do you know?"

"Oh, doctors can pick runners out of crowd," he said. "It's the blood pressure and heart rate. That doesn't happen by accident."

Financial margin doesn't happen by accident either. If you define your current reality, define what you want your reality to be, and protect new margin rather than spending it, you can have peace of mind and confidence that you can handle whatever financial stress life throws at you.

CHAPTER 5

Prepare for the Best

As a financial advisor, sometimes I have to help my clients come out of denial and embrace a reality that they are avoiding. It's one of the most difficult challenges to overcome, but there are many times when I have to be the voice of reason when people just don't want to face the truth. When this happens, I have to make sure I have all the facts lined up, all the documentation that proves my point, and all the charts and graphs that lead to the irrefutable reality before I deliver the sobering news:

You guys are doing really, really well.

I've come to see that people don't do an adequate job of preparing for the best and I've also seen that this can lead to some of life's biggest regrets. When we don't prepare for the best, we can miss the best when it comes our way. It often takes a while for the magnitude of the regrets to sink in. Sometimes it doesn't happen until the twilight years of life when people realize they could have retired five years earlier, or they could have taken the trips they wanted to take, or spent more time with family and friends. Helping people prepare for the best is one of the most challenging but also one of the most rewarding parts of my job — and it usually starts with some basic questions. When you were younger, what did you promise yourself or promise your spouse that you would do at this point in your life? Are you doing that? If not, why not?

Cross Your Heart

It's hard to believe that a cartoon can bring a grown man to tears, but the first twelve minutes of the movie Up are some of the most emotionally-charged scenes I've ever watched. Two young kids, Carl and Ellie, meet and form The Spirit of Adventure club. Their motto is "Adventure is Out There." Ellie shows Carl her top secret "My Adventure Book," filled with all the dreams of things she will do when she is older. She makes Carl promise to take her to Paradise Falls in South America on a blimp when they grow up. She even makes him cross his heart.

When they are older, Carl and Ellie fall in love and get married, and they still have the same adventurous dreams. But it seems each time they get close to taking that trip something stops them. Then, in their twilight years, Carl realizes he never kept his promise. So he goes to the travel agency and books the trip to South America, and puts the tickets in a picnic basket to surprise Ellie. On the way to the picnic, however, Ellie collapses. They waited too long. And even though he crossed his heart, Ellie's adventure book will never have pictures of the two of them in Paradise Falls.

I think this opening sequence is so moving because we all have unique dreams of what we would like to do if we ever get the chance. And there is something in us that knows that when we have missed the opportunity to live out our dreams, something precious and irreplaceable has been lost. And yet, time and time again I have watched people talk themselves out of their dreams even though their dreams are perfectly in reach.

Like Mark and Cheryl Freise, two of my favorite clients. Ten years earlier, when they were fifty-five years old, they shared a dream with me.

"We've always said that when we're sixty-five, we want to take a trip around the world." It was fun to see their eyes light up when they talked about it. Adventure is out there! Mark and Cheryl were serious about this, so we made it part of their retirement plan. Now, ten years later, it was time for the dream to come true.

"So, when are you going to book that trip?" I asked. I could tell the question made them uneasy. "What's wrong?"

"Well," they said, "in order to take that trip we would have to take money out of our retirement account."

It was as if they had said, "To take that trip we will have to commit an unthinkable crime!" I had to laugh.

"But you're retired!" I said, "What did you think that retirement account was for? Why did you save that money in your retirement account if weren't going to use it in your retirement?"

Even though they had done a great job with their retirement plan, and even though they had actually done better than they had hoped financially, Mark and Cheryl were talking themselves out of their dream.

Why do we talk ourselves out of our dreams? Why aren't we ready for the best that life has to offer when it comes our way?

The Ceiling and the Floor

One of the reasons we have a hard time preparing for the best has to do with our financial ceilings and floors. Here's what I mean. Imagine you are huge NFL fan just starting out in life and you tell yourself, "If I had a hundred thousand dollars in the bank, I would use part of it to go to the Super Bowl." A hundred-thousand dollars is your ceiling because it's just a dream. Then you spend years working and saving, and you slowly build a nest egg of a hundred thousand dollars. But now it's no longer your dream ceiling. Now it's your floor. It's what you're standing on. It's what you depend on. You can't spend any part of that hundred thousand dollars, because then you wouldn't have a hundred thousand dollars anymore.

Here's what you tell yourself: "If I had another hundred thousand dollars, then I would go to the Super Bowl." And the cycle repeats. Here's what I have seen to be true in people's emotional stance towards their money:

Your ceiling always becomes your next floor.

It doesn't matter how much money you have, and it doesn't matter if it's more money than you ever dreamed of having. Every time you get to the most money you've ever had in your life, it becomes simply the money that you now have. Not only that, but you've already become used to having that much money. It's what feels familiar, and it's what makes you feel safe. And if it goes below what you now have, you're somehow going backwards. People get stuck in this circular reasoning that "I have to have that much money because that's how much money I have." I often have conversations that go like this:

"I can't spend that money. I need it."
"Explain to me why you need it."
"Because if I spend it, I won't have that much money anymore."
"Yes, but why do have to have that much money?"
"Because it is what I have."

It is completely illogical, but the emotional barrier to getting past this reasoning is strong. That's why people find it so easy to talk themselves out of their dreams. It has nothing to do with financial security and everything to do with breaking out of this faulty reasoning and the emotional dependence on their current floor.

The ceiling and floor issue is an obstacle during our earning years. It becomes a minefield when we retire. If it's hard to give up some of your floor when you have the ability to earn it back, think about how hard it is to give up some of your floor when there is no more salary coming in. So here's the irony: When we cross the threshold into retirement — the years when we say we're really going to live out our dreams — we have the most difficulty spending money. What if things don't go as well as we planned next year? What if more of our floor disappears? We have an easy time assuming that the worst will happen, and we scare ourselves into thinking that things could get really bad really fast.

What If You're Wrong?

When I'm trying to help my clients to keep those promises that they made to themselves, this is the pushback I get most often.

"What if you're wrong? What if things don't go the way we're planning they will go next year?"

It's a good question, because I might be wrong. I've been wrong before, and I'm pretty sure I'll be wrong again. But I won't be that wrong. And even if I'm wrong this year, I won't be wrong over the next 30 years. More to the point, if I am wrong, we will adjust in real-time. If next year is not as good as we had planned, we might have to tighten the belt for a while. Real life doesn't travel in a straight line, and that's okay. We don't need to overreact to the ups and downs.

I turn the question around for my clients to consider.

"So if I'm wrong, we adjust. But what if you're wrong? If you're wrong, the only option you have is regret. If I'm wrong, we can fix that problem quickly, but if you're wrong, you've wasted an opportunity to live out your dream that you might not be able to get back."

I spend a lot of time wondering why people get so focused on the fear that I might be wrong. Why is it so easy for them to imagine that we've planned on a seven percent return on investment next year, and they might make less — or even worse, they could lose money — so they will be financially ruined and have to eat spam for the rest of their lives?

One day, the answer hit me: It's because that's the fear they practice. They have practiced over and over again what it would feel like if I'm wrong. I know they have played out that movie in their minds time and time again and have imagined every possible tragic ending. They have practiced what each of those tragic endings feels like.

What they've never practiced, not even once, is what it would feel like if they're wrong. They've never imagined the movie ending where they are 90 and have $8,000,000 but haven't done a single item on their bucket list. They are never afraid of this movie ending, and they should be — because this is the one you can't recover from. This is why I'm so passionate about helping people prepare for the best. I don't have to imagine this ending; I've seen it so often. People always assume they will have more time, they always assume they will feel better about spending money in the future, and then one day it's just too late. One day, they realize their story is coming to an end, and it doesn't include any scenes where they are living out their dreams with the people they love.

Here is the rule of thumb that I use to help my clients prepare for the best and actually spend the money that they have planned on spending to live out their dreams.

You plan to be at point x at a point in time and then follow these guidelines:

- If you are at point x plus some, you are totally free to spend what we planned for you to spend plus some of the extra.

- If you are at point x, you are totally free to spend what we had planned for you to spend.

- If you are at point x minus some, you are still probably okay in spending what we had planned for you to spend. There's no reason to overreact to a little blip in the plan. If it will make you feel more comfortable to spend a little less, that's okay as well.

People are sometimes shocked when my advice about that unexpected windfall is to spend it. They usually assume that a financial advisor will always tell them to invest it. They assume that I will judge myself by how big of a pool of money I can help them accumulate before they die. But that's not what I care about, and it's not what I want them to care about. I want them to care about having the most richly satisfying life with the least regrets possible. That's why if they've already done all the investing we had planned for the year and they are right on track with their goals, my inclination is to say "Adventure is out there!" Go live your life. Do something meaningful with that money. Spend it. Give it to your kids. Put it in your Abundance Fund and give it away. Or sock it away, but only sock it away because you don't have a better idea.

Lavish

Sometimes people don't live out their dreams because it just feels too lavish. We feel guilty spending all that money on ourselves, or we worry about what other people will think about us. Will they think we are shallow or self-centered? Sometimes it just feels more prudent to give up on our dreams. It feels wiser to live a life that no one can criticize. To escape criticism, we sacrifice the shared experiences that make our lives rich — and it's one of the worst trade-offs we can make.

Shared Experiences Versus Things

There are a lot of people who find it almost impossible to spend money to live out their dreams, but they won't think twice about spending that money on things. They will redo the kitchen or buy a new car or the latest computer without blinking an eye. If they have something physical in return, it feels like they are not wasting their money because there is something of value to show for it.

In the world of money and regret, this thinking is backwards. The more familiar you are with something, the less valuable it becomes to you. When you buy the latest phone with all the new buttons, or the latest refrigerator with all of the new advances in technology, it can be very exciting. It's all so new! But three weeks later, that phone with all the new buttons is just your phone, and that expensive refrigerator is just the place you put your groceries after you shop. You become so familiar with it so quickly that it's really nothing special.

The exact opposite happens when we spend our money on shared experiences. The further away you get from that trip to Paris, the less familiar you are with the experience. You try to keep the memories fresh by taking pictures and videos or keeping a vacation journal, but with each year that passes, the memories of that trip become less and less familiar and more and more precious to you.

The material experience of the average American has never been this good. Across all income levels, we have more stuff than we've ever had: more possessions, more entertainment, more information, and more square footage in our homes. And yet on a happiness scale, we are as unhappy as we've ever been. Money spent on more stuff will not provide the same value as money spent creating connection with the people you love through shared experiences.

That's why, when death is nearing and people look back on their lives, what they think about most is the shared experiences they've had with the people that they love, or the shared experiences that they've let pass by. They think about how magical that second honeymoon was, or how fun it was to be at their grandchildren's weddings. Or they think about how they wish they wouldn't have waited until it was too late to do the road trip across America, or how they wish they wouldn't have allowed financial worry to keep them from spending more Christmases with their children. Nobody ever dies thinking, "I really wish I would have added another room to the house" or "I'm so glad I had the latest iPhone in 2012." In the economy of money and regret, shared experiences become more valuable over time, and things become less valuable.

Things, it turns out, are only valuable if they are connected with shared experiences. I had a client who purchased some property on the gulf coast, but she only bought it so there would be a place for her children and grandchildren to get together every year. This year, they had their fifth reunion, and she told me that not only was it fun creating new shared experiences, but she was amazed at how much fun it was for everyone to share memories of the previous four years. All week long, she would hear things like:

"Hey, do you remember when we went fishing and little Jimmy hooked that Marlin? What did he name it? I thought I was going to die laughing."

"Remember when we went to the fireworks and they accidentally set off every firework in the first ten seconds?"

"Remember when the power went out and we had to light candles, and we sat around telling ghost stories? We should do that again!"

Shared experiences become shared memories that connect us deeply to the people who matter most.

The Future You

There is one other problem I've seen with preparing for the best: you don't know who you are going to be 30 years from now.

Remember Mark and Cheryl Freise, the couple who promised themselves that they were going to take a trip around the world? As I helped them gain the confidence that they could make their dream come true, another problem surfaced.

Cheryl had been building up sky miles her entire career as a traveling saleswoman, and naturally they thought this would help them on their world tour. What Cheryl didn't know was that her 65-year-old self would never want to step on another plane as long as she lived. She had come to hate airports, and wasn't too crazy about staying in a different hotel every few days either. Mark, on the other hand, hadn't been able to travel as much and had spent years dreaming of flying to Europe and Asia.

Sometimes we change over the years, and we either need to come up with new dreams, or come up with new ways to live out the old dream. In this case, it was Cheryl who came up with the solution.

"What if we take a world cruise?"

Mark liked that idea even more than flying. So they booked the tickets and were gone almost a whole year. Six months later, I got an email from Cheryl who was on a ship half-way around the world.

Thanks so much for not letting us give up on our dream. I cannot tell you much fun we are having. These memories will last a lifetime. There's no way we would have come if you hadn't held us to our promise to each other.

Dreaming with Confidence

I want you to know that it is possible for you to not only live out your dreams, but to enjoy those moments with abandon. Throw yourself into them with all that is in you. There are three steps you can begin to take today to make sure that you are prepared for the best.

The first step is to cross your heart. Set a date to talk to the people who matter most to you about the shared experiences that you want to have in life. Figure out what your non-negotiables will be, and decide together that you are going to value shared experiences over things.

The second step is to have a plan. I'm guessing that in the movie *Up*, the real reason Carl and Ellie never made it to Paradise Falls was that they had a change jar instead of a financial plan. Without a plan, you can never be sure if your spending is wildly reckless or overlyaustere.

The third step is to get a financial advisor who will hold you accountable to your dreams. Even with a solid plan, you will have difficulty feeling confident enough to spend money on shared experiences if you don't have someone who will tell you to buy the tickets and go.

It's your life. It's your dreams. It's your story. So cross your heart, get a plan, and get someone who won't let you miss the best when it's in your reach.

Adventure is out there.

CHAPTER 6

Prepare for the Worst

I know. This is the chapter that you are tempted to skip. Talking about preparing for the worst means talking about the fact that things might not go as well as you hope. Every now and then, life is going to throw something at us we don't expect, and sometimes those things can be devastating if we don't prepare for them. Can you feel yourself wanting to get as far away from this book as you can right now? Avoidance is the natural human reaction to these topics, but avoidance also leads to life-shattering regrets.

So here's my goal in this chapter. I want to lay out a simple plan so that one month from today, you have done most of the heavy lifting in preparing for the worst and rarely have to think about it again. Along the way we will notice the reasons why we want to avoid this subject and I will give you shortcuts through the maze that will put you in control of the process. How does that sound? Can you stick with me for ten pages?

Here is the big problem with the regret of not preparing for the worst. With the other regrets we have talked about, we can feel them building slowly over time. You can feel it building when you are getting into credit card debt, or when you are trading relationships for money. But the regret that comes from not preparing for the worst doesn't exist until someone dies or becomes disabled, and when it does show up the level of damage is infinitely higher than a little too much credit card debt or skipping a vacation. It's devastating, but it's also invisible until it's too late.

In this chapter, we are going to talk about the three big what-ifs: What if I die? What if I become too sick or injured to work? What if I lose my job? Each of these has the potential to cause significant harm to ourselves and the people that we love, and to cause significant regret. And with each, we can take simple steps to minimize the risk of regret. Let's deal with the big one first.

What If I Die?

In the world of money and regret, if you die, the people that you love will lose three things: they will lose your income, your protection, and your guidance. That's a lot to lose. When you prepare for the worst, you come as close as you can to ensuring that your loved ones will still have your income, protection, and guidance long after you are gone.

Losing Your Income

The way you ensure they still have income is to purchase life insurance. I get it — there are lots of reasons we don't want to talk about life insurance. One of the main reasons is the way that it's sold. There always seems to be a high-pressure agent that's more concerned with his commission than your protection, steering you in a direction that you don't want to go. We know the agent has a conflict of interest, and he wants to sell us the product that will make him the most money. This can be such a miserable process that we just avoid it. Another reason we don't want to think about life insurance is we don't want to think about our own mortality. So let's make this as easy as possible, because here's what I want for you: One month from today, as you are kissing your spouse goodnight or tucking your kids into bed, I want you to have the confidence that if the worst happens, they will be taken care of.

Let's start with rule number one of buying insurance: the purpose of insurance is to transfer risk. For example, if your house burns down, you would not be able to afford to pay to have it rebuilt. That's a risk. So, you pay an insurance company a certain amount each month on the really unlikely chance that it might burn down, so if it does, they assume all the risk of paying to have it rebuilt.

It's the same with having life insurance. If you or your spouse dies, your family will be without that income. That's risky. You pay an insurance company a certain amount each month so that if one of you dies, the insurance company assumes all the risk of making up the lost income. You no longer have to worry about that risk.

Let me say this again: For the purposes of this chapter, the only purpose of buying insurance is to transfer risk. I don't want to get into the debate of the different kinds of life insurance here. Insurance companies have a variety of products that they might try to sell you. Some of them transfer a part of your risk and also do other things. Here is your shortcut through the maze — the only thing you need is to transfer the risk of losing your income. Any other side benefit is secondary. If there is a compelling reason for you to have a side benefit, that's up to you. But if it doesn't transfer all of your risk for the least amount of money possible, it's not what you need. Ignoring this can be devastating.

Alonzo loved his wife and kids very much, but Alonzo wasn't really prepared for the worst when he died from a heart attack at the age of 35. Alonzo even had life insurance. The problem was that he was more concerned with the cash value of his insurance than he was about the death benefit. He was more focused on the side benefit than covering the risk of losing his income if he died. So, he had $50,000 worth of life insurance for which he paid over $100 a month because he wanted his life insurance to also be a savings account. He could have easily had a half a million dollars' worth of life insurance that would have cost him around $30 a month, but that's not what he did. When the insurance company delivered the $50,000 check to his wife, Rosa, she knew it would barely be enough to cover one year of Alonzo's income, let alone the next nineteen years until his three daughters would be out of college and on their own. I met her a year after her husband's death, and that's when, in a moment of brutal honesty, she said perhaps the single most motivating sentence I've ever heard when it comes to preparing for the worst.

"I loved Alonzo very much," she told me, "and I still miss him. But there are times I get so angry about the situation he left us in that I wish I could dig him up and kill him again."

I know she was exaggerating. But I also know she was speaking out of a place of intense pain that was avoidable. Here's the hard truth. Dying wasn't the worst thing that happened to Alonzo. Dying and leaving his family crippled by financial stress was the worst thing that happened.

And the tragedy is it would have been so easy to prepare for the worst. Let's walk through how simple the process can be. The first step in buying insurance is to figure how much you need and for how long you need it. You don't want your insurance agent telling you how much you need any more than you want a bank telling you how much house you can afford. There is an inherent conflict of interest because the more they sell you, the more they will make. You can take control of the process by already knowing what you need before you begin shopping.

So how much insurance do you need? My rule of thumb is that you should have around ten times your annual income in term life insurance. If you have a financial plan and already know exactly how much you are planning to spend twenty years from now, you will be able to fine-tune that number. You may only need eight times your annual income, or you might need twelve times. But ten times is a good rule of thumb to start with.

So, how long will you need it? The general rule of thumb here is that you will need it until your children are through college and out on their own. After that, the risk of your family not having your income will be lower because they will have their own income at that point.

So let's say you figure out that you need $500,000 worth of death benefit for twenty years. How do you go about getting that insurance?

First, you call your insurance agent or you go to one of online companies and let them know you want a twenty-year term life insurance policy worth half a million dollars. They will give you a comically low monthly payment like $30 a month — really, it's just not that expensive — and you make your first payment at that time. The insurance company will do their underwriting and send a nurse out to your house to take blood and urine samples so they can evaluate your health, and you will answer a lot of medical questions. By the time that first month is done, you've got an answer from the insurance company saying one of three things. They will say you are approved as applied for, which means you continue paying $30 each month. Or they will say you are approved other than as applied for because they've seen a health issue and let you know the policy will be

$45 or $60 a month. Most of the time, you take it because the same issues will show up no matter who does the testing. The third option is they decline you and they give you your $30 back. Once you have determined what you need and make that initial call or fill out online application, the ball is rolling and all you do is respond to the insurance company.

To recap: First, you figure out what you need and how long you need it. Then you call your agent or go online and tell the insurance company exactly what you want to get the process started. Finally, just do what the insurance company asks you to do to complete the process. Not that complicated, the part you initiate takes about five minutes, and the entire process will only take about a month. You can start as soon as you finish reading this chapter.

Losing Your Protection

The second thing your family loses if you die is your protection. If you have children, you are their guardian, so you make all the decisions that protect their interests. If you and your spouse die, your children lose that protection. The way you prepare for the worst in case your children lose your protection is to create a will. When you create a will, you decide in advanced who will do the best job protecting your children's interests, and you make sure that they become your children's guardians in your place. If you don't have a will, the state will decide who takes care of your kids. They may assign them to Uncle Bob, even though the kids hate him or have no relationship with him. It would have been so much better if it was Aunt Sally, but the state doesn't know that if you don't have a will.

The other reason to establish a will is to ensure the assets go to the right person. Many people assume that if they die, their spouse automatically gets everything they own, but that's not necessarily true. Many states have complicated rules to determine who gets what when there is no will, and it may not be the person the deceased would have wanted. Fortunately, it's quick and easy to get a basic will that says, "Here's who we want to be guardian of our kids, and if one of us dies the other spouse gets everything." It takes two meetings. You will meet with the lawyer first to let her know what you want. You will meet again once the will is drawn up to sign it. It will cost about three to five-hundred dollars, and you will have ensured that the people you love have their interests protected in case the worst happens.

Most legal firms have someone who handles simple wills. If you know a lawyer, even if she is not an estate attorney, you can ask her to refer you to the person in her firm who handles wills. If you don't, you can contact a few law firms near you to see what they charge for creating a simple will and go from there.

I would stay away from online sites where you can write your own will without the help of a lawyer. With a lawyer, you not only have a higher degree of ensuring the will is exactly what you want, but you and your family have someone who can be held financially responsible if there is a mistake in the will. If there is a mistake in the will you draw up without a lawyer, you're stuck with it.

Losing Your Guidance

The final thing your family loses if you die is your guidance. You won't be there to give advice about paying for college, or buying that first car or home, or saving for retirement. That's a lot to lose. If you leave a large amount of money, then it's not enough just to provide for the loss of your income. If little Johnny gets $500,000 when he turns eighteen, then little Johnny is going to get a Porsche. Little Johnny will also take a few of his closest friends to Cabo for a month. It won't take long before little Johnny blows through all of his money. Think of it this way: The more money you leave for the people you love, the more they are going to miss your guidance in how to make the best financial decisions with that money.

The way you prepare for the worst when the people you love lose your guidance is to create a trust. That's what Ben did. When I met Ben, he was already dying of cancer. His wife had died ten years earlier, and he had an eighteen-year-old daughter named Candice. Ben lived a couple more years after I met him, and in that time we created a trust to help Candace make the best use of the money that he was going to leave her.

One day, Candace came in to talk to me.

"I'm trying to figure out if I should buy a house and how that works," she said. So I walked her through the math and helped her figure out how much she could spend each month and still have plenty of margin. It was within the parameters of the trust for her to use some of the money to make the down payment and I told her I thought that was a good idea. Then we started to talk about the process of buying a house.

That's when she broke down and started crying. "What's wrong?" I asked, a little taken aback.

"You don't understand," she said. "This is what a dad would do. This is the kind of conversation that someone who has a dad would just take for granted. I don't get to talk to my dad, but you knew my dad. You're telling me what he would tell me. You're the closest thing I have to a dad."

It was a profoundly moving moment for me. I felt honored, but I also felt so glad that her father had made that moment possible for her. It was the best thing that could have happened after the worst happened.

When you set up a trust, there are two main questions you will need to answer. The first is who will be the successor trustee — the person in charge of releasing funds. When choosing a trustee, you are looking for two main qualities: Someone who has proven themselves to be financially responsible and someone who knows and loves your kids. They don't have to be a relative. In reality, you will choose multiple successor trustees. The first successor will be your spouse, the second will take over if your spouse dies, the third will be someone to take over if that person dies, and so on.

I strongly recommend that the person you name as the trustee is different than the person you name as guardian. You want to make sure that the purse strings are controlled by someone who is not benefitting from the money. You don't want a guardian-trustee in position of adding on to their house because it's kind of for the kids. It's better for everyone if those two responsibilities stay separate. However, the trustee and the guardian should be people who know each other, interact with each other regularly, and work well together.

The second question your lawyer will help you with is how long you are going to protect little Johnny from himself. For example, your kids may get a third of the money when they graduate from college, another third when they turn 30, and the final balance when they turn 30-five. Your lawyer will help you figure out how to stage that based on your circumstances. Once those stages are set, your kids will automatically get that money at those milestones, and they can do whatever they want with it. The trustee can release funds to them sooner if it's within the guidelines of the trust. For example, if Johnny graduates and decides to go to medical school, it might be within the parameters of the trust to release funds early to make that happen. If Johnny gets married and wants to purchase a house, that also might be within the purpose of the trust.

When you call the lawyer to create a will, you can let them know if you also need their help in creating a trust. Even if you create a trust, you will still need a will. But you can start both of those processes at the same time.

What If I Become Sick or Injured and Can't Work?

If you are out of work because you are sick or injured, you experience a double whammy. You lose your income because you are no longer working, but you also increase your expenses because of the care you need to recover from your sickness or injury.

Being sick or injured is not easy. If you do become sick or injured, you want to be able to spend your emotional energy on getting well; you don't need the added stress of being in a financial nightmare. I've talked with many couples who have gone through this. I've seen the resentment towards the person who got hurt. I've seen the mutual blame, and I've heard the private thoughts. "It would have been better if I had just died. Then at least my family would have got a million bucks. But I lived and they got nothing but trouble. I get to wake up and think of that every day." You can imagine the kind of stress this creates for even the most committed couples.

The way you prepare for the worst if you get sick or injured and cannot work is to purchase long-term disability insurance. How much disability insurance do you need? The answer is easy: as much as you can get. Most companies will insure up to 80% of your current salary. And you will need it. Remember rule number one of purchasing insurance? The only purpose of insurance is to transfer risk. So let's think about the risk that you need to have covered by your disability insurance.

First, there is the risk of not being able to pay for your monthly expenses. Second, there is the risk of not being able to pay for the care you need when you are in recovery. Third, there is the risk of not being able to save for retirement. Don't overlook this last point. Most long-term policies end when you reach the age of 65, which means you're still going to need a retirement account. And you might still have to pay taxes on the money you receive (if you pay the premium, the benefit is not taxed; if your company pays the premium, it is taxed). That's why I always recommend getting as much disability insurance as you can.

Don't automatically assume that the disability insurance you get from work covers everything you need. Sometimes people will tell me, "I don't need much more disability insurance, because my employer will replace 60% of my income."

Then I'll look at the policy and say "No, they will replace 60% up to $2000 a month, and you make

$10,000 a month! That's only a 20% replacement, so you need a lot more."

The steps to getting disability insurance are also pretty simple. You want to talk to your employer first to see how much disability insurance you have, and if you can get more. Getting it through your employer is probably cheaper, so you want to maximize that resource first. Next, when you call your insurance agent to purchase life insurance, you also ask how much disability insurance they will sell you. It's easiest to do both together. If you're calling for disability insurance the same time you call for life insurance, they will use the same blood and urine sample. In addition to the medical tests and questions involved in getting life insurance, they will also ask for documents to determine how much money you make, and how much disability insurance you already have. Once they have finished, they will give you a quote on how much they will sell you and how much it will cost.

There is one more risk involved in getting sick or injured. There is a risk that you might become so incapacitated that you won't be able to make personal health decisions or financial decisions. If that happens, you want to make sure you know who is going to be making those decisions. You also want your spouse to be able to sign checks and do the other things he or she needs to do. The way you prepare for the worst in this case is to have a Power of Attorney. This is also not a hard fix. When you call the lawyer asking for a will, you also let her know that you want her to create a Power of Attorney.

What If I Lose My Job?

If you lose your job, you will not have income to pay your expenses until you get a new job. The way you minimize the risk of losing a job is having an emergency fund equal to three to six months' worth of expenses. I wish I could tell you that I had a simple step to help you have three to six months' worth of expenses saved up in a month, but I don't. This one will take a little bit longer. You can take a look at your spending plan and decide how much you will set aside each month to create this emergency fund, and you can get that in place this month so you don't have to think about it any longer.

One Month Away

Sometimes my clients can get pretty shaken up when we meet and they think we are going to talk about investing and creating wealth, and we let them know that we can't begin any of that work because they don't have a will, or don't have the insurance that they need. I won't do any of that work with them until I know they are prepared for the worst. As I walk them through the reasons the reaction is the same. "How could we have missed this?" Even though we hate dealing with this subject and are prone to avoid it, all you really have to do is three things:

- Call an insurance agent and let them know how much term life insurance you want and for how long. Ask them how much long-term disability you can get.

- Call a lawyer and tell them you want to create a simple will and Power of Attorney documents, and set up the appointment for the first meeting. Let them know if you will also need their help in creating a trust.

- Have a conversation with your spouse and decide how much you will put in your emergency fund each month in case one of you loses your job.

You can do these three simple steps this week, and once you do, you are one month away from being prepared for the worst.

CHAPTER 7

Don't Make Every Financial Decision About the Numbers

If you were a fly on the wall of my office, you might hear me say something like this to one of my clients who is trying to make a difficult decision:

"If we look at the math, there is no way this decision makes sense. We can run the numbers all day long and they will say the same thing. But I think you should do it anyway. In fact, if you don't spend this money, I think it might be one of the biggest regrets of your life."

It's not what people expect to hear from their financial advisor. People expect to hear that math is king, and you should always do what the numbers tell you to do. But there are times when math is not king. And being able to spot the moments when math is not king is critical to living a rich life.

This was true for Clark and Tonya Jennings. They believed that what they wanted to do was probably a complete waste of money, so they were almost apologetic for even taking up my time by coming into my office and talking about it.

"I know what you're going to say," Clark started, "but we just wanted to make sure that we weren't missing something." "Sure," I said, "what's going on?"

"It's about our daughter and her husband. They've been trying to have children for five years now and haven't been able to. They have a specialist who has been helping them, but nothing has worked to this point. They've spent a lot of money on this, and they're at a point where they just can't afford to keep trying."

"There is another treatment they could try" said Tonya, "but it's very expensive, and there is no guarantee that it would work."

"It's twenty-five thousand dollars," Clark said. "That's a lot of money to bet on a longshot. I know it sounds ridiculous, but we were thinking about offering to pay for the treatment. We just can't get past the idea that it's a really bad financial decision."

"Well," I said, "I don't think you've missed anything on the financial side. I think you're seeing things pretty clearly. But there's something else I need to know. How important is it to you that your daughter is able to have children? How much do you want grandchildren?"

Neither answered and, after a moment, I realized it was because they were both trying to regain their composure enough to answer the question. They had become too emotional to speak, and I knew we had come to the heart of the matter.

"You know," I said, "this decision isn't about the numbers. I know it might feel like you're wasting money, but you're not. This is money you have to spend. If you don't try this, you'll be wondering about what could have been for the rest of your life."

Don't get me wrong. Numbers are great. I'm in a numbers business. I always want to know what the math says. But I've also seen that big regrets arrive when people focus on the math and don't follow their hearts. That's what Clark and Tonya were doing. They were so concerned with the financial ramifications of the decision that they weren't fully connected with what their hearts were telling them.

Blinders

Horses have almost 360° peripheral vision. They can see everything except for what is right in front of their nose and what is right behind their tail. However, when horses race or pull wagons or carriages, people often fit them with blinders that prevent them from seeing what is beside or behind them. This reduces their vision to as little as 30 degrees, and allows them to perform without being distracted or panicked because of other things going on around them.

I've been struck by how often, when it comes to making financial decisions, math can become the blinders that keep people from seeing the big picture. There is something about running the financial projections for a decision that prevents people from connecting on an emotional level with the things that matter most to them — with the things that lead to a rich life.

Financial prudence is a good thing. It's usually helpful to play it safe and avoid as much risk as possible. But every once in a while, an opportunity will come your way that is so central to what it means for you to live a rich life that taking a risk is the right choice. Every once in a while, you have to swing for the fences.

There are two questions I ask my clients to help them know when it's time to ignore the math and swing for the fences. The first question is this: *If money wasn't an object, what decision would you make?* Now, I know we all have limitations, and I know that we can't do everything we want to do. But that's not the point. The point is that by taking the math out of the equation, we are taking off our blinders. This allows us to see the big picture so we can get to the heart of the decision.

Consider Ray, who was twenty years into his corporate career. Ray had a heart condition and an anxiety disorder and both his doctor and his therapist had suggested that he consider a career change — and not because his job was too hard. Ray could handle hard. They suggested the career change because he was miserable. There was nothing about his job that he enjoyed. It sucked the life out of him, and it was impacting his physical and emotional health. In working with his therapist, he came up with two different career options. The problem was they both payed less than half of his current salary. Ray balked at making such a drastic change. He wanted to stay at his current job for fifteen more years, then retire and do something else. His therapist kept pressing, though, and that was when Ray came to me for moral support. He was certain that the numbers guy would agree with him.

He told me about the other jobs and the difference in salary. He told me what the difference in pay would do to his investment plans and his retirement. All he talked about was the numbers. "Ray," I said, "let me ask you a question. Do you want to keep doing your current job?"

He looked confused for a moment, as though I hadn't been paying attention. He started over with his outline of the financial impact of the potential change.

"I get the math, Ray," I said. "I get that one hundred and fifty thousand dollars is more than sixty thousand dollars. That's not what I asked. What I asked was, 'Do you want to keep doing your current job?'"

Again, he looked confused, as if the sentence didn't make sense. So I tried again.

"Let's assume for a moment that money wasn't an object. If all three jobs payed the same, *would you want to change careers?*"

"In a heartbeat," he said, perhaps surprising himself at how quick and forceful his answer was.

"Why?"

"Are you kidding?" he said. "I would love either of those jobs. It would actually be fun to get out of bed in the morning."

"Here's the problem, Ray," I said. "I think the difference in pay between those jobs is blinding you to the most important parts of this decision. I don't think the option of working fifteen more years at your current job and then having an amazing retirement is actually available to you. I think you will burn out — or worse. Even if you somehow survive fifteen years at that job, you're going to be dragging yourself to the finish line. Your retirement is not going to be what you're hoping for. Besides that, I think your wife and kids would rather have a happy, healthy version of you come home every night than a version that is always at risk of a heart attack."

The 30-Year Rule

The second question I ask my clients to help them know when it's time to ignore the math and swing for the fences is this: Is this decision going to matter to you 30 years from now? The 30-year rule will help you understand when it's okay to risk money in order to live a richer life. This is the conversation that I had with Clark and Tonya when they were wondering if they should spend the money to help their daughter have children.

"30 years from now, how will you view this decision? If you spend the money and have grandchildren, will you be glad that you decided to help? If you spend the money and don't get grandchildren, will you be glad that you at least tried? If you don't spend the money, 30 years from now, will you wish you had taken the chance, or will you be glad that you have the money?"

It was a no-brainer for them at that point. It was obvious to them that this wasn't a time to play it safe. This was a moment to swing for the fences.

Today, Clark and Tonya have two beautiful grand-daughters who are the delight of their lives. They love watching their daughter be a mom. Their lives, which were already rich, are so much more full with those two little girls as part of the family. Clark and Tonya are grateful that they didn't miss the opportunity to swing for the fences, but I know that even if things hadn't worked out the way they had wanted, they would have never regretted taking the chance.

The 30-year rule was also helpful to Ray. It was clear that if he didn't make a change, he wouldn't even be alive in 30 years. So for the past eight years, he's been teaching high school science and coaching the robotics team at his school. We had to change his financial plan because of the change in salary. Retiring at 55 was not going to work, so now he plans to retire at 60. But he is experiencing a much richer life now instead of waiting until he finally drags himself over the finish line and is too beat up to enjoy whatever time he has left. His next twenty years are going to be immeasurably better, so the five year trade-off in retirement is well worth it.

The Flip Side

The two questions will help you do what is important to you even when the numbers don't recommend it, and they will also help you do the opposite. They will help you follow your gut and avoid doing things even when the numbers say it's okay. That's the situation that Bruce and Danielle found themselves in. Their son is an entrepreneur, and he asked Bruce and Danielle for some money that would allow him to pay off his credit card debt and do a major expansion in his business. He was convinced that this would solve all his problems. But they were struggling with whether or not to help.

"Let's take the math out of this for a moment," I said. "Let's say you had unlimited finances. If that were the case, would you want to give him the money?"

"I don't think so," said Danielle. She was a little hesitant because they had been my clients long enough that they had an abundance fund, and they shared my value of generosity.

"And actually," she said, "from a strictly numbers point of view, we can afford to give him the money. It's not a big enough number that we would have to make any major changes to our financial plan."

I think she expected me to tell them to go ahead and give their son the money. Instead, I asked the second question.

"In 30 years, will this decision matter to you? Will you be glad you didn't help him out of his current problem? Or will you wish you had given him the money instead."

"Honestly," said Bruce, "It's really hard to say "no" to him right now. We have the money, and he knows we have the money. The easiest thing right now is to help him out. But in 30 years, I think we'll be much happier if we say no.

"I agree," said Danielle, "He has a habit of overextending himself. I'm afraid that if we bail him out, he'll overextend himself even more and be further into debt. At some point, he has to learn to live within limits, and that might mean he has to dig himself out of this problem he's created."

"You know," said Bruce, "I was really about to cave in and just give him the money. But thinking about how we'll view this 30 years from now puts it in the right perspective. But it's still going to be really hard to turn him down."

"Well," I said, "one of the advantages of having a financial advisor is you can just blame me. I happen to agree with you 100%, so you can tell your son that your financial advisor said it was not a good decision at this time."

I was happy to be the bad guy if that would help my clients and their son in the long run.

The Smokescreen

Sometimes the math involved in a decision can be a set of blinders that keeps us from seeing the big picture. But I've noticed that sometimes the numbers are a smokescreen to hide the real reason we are making a decision.

Here's the most recent example. A client of mine named Finney told me he was thinking about buying a new car.

"The mechanic said it's going to cost $2000 dollars to get the car fixed. That's way too much money to put in that old car. It just makes more sense financially to get a new car."

Did you notice the smokescreen? Did you notice what he was hiding?

"Stop right there," I interrupted. "There is no way you're going to convince me from a numbers perspective that paying a $3,000 down payment and having a $320 monthly payment for the next five years is less costly than a $2,000 repair. There is no universe in which that math works out. Just admit you want a new car. You're tired of driving the clunker and want something nice. It's okay to want nice things."

I can usually tell when someone is using a smokescreen, because the math involved is really bad math. We use it to hide from ourselves and others that the real reason we are buying something is because *we want it!* It's like we're saying, "I wouldn't have made this decision except it just made so much sense from a numbers perspective."

I hear this kind of bad math all the time. In fact, I think the bad math smokescreen has almost become a sacred pact in our society. We all know when someone is using a smokescreen. We've just decided that if you don't call me out when I say I bought the new car because it saved me so much money in the long run, I won't call you out when you say you bought the new sofa because the twelve months same as cash offer was too good to pass by. But even though we've made this sacred pact not to notice each other's smokescreens, these can still be really bad decisions that lead to regret.

So whenever I see one of my clients using their smokescreen, I ask the two questions.

"Finney, let's take the financial side out of the equation. If money were no object, would you repair the old car or buy the new car?

"I'd get the new car, of course."

Taking the numbers out of the equation helps us connect with our hearts. It helps us to know what we want. But we still have to figure out if we can afford what we want, and that's where the second question comes in.

"Will you care in 30 years if you drove your old car three more years? Will you care if instead of buying a brand new car, you bought a car with sixty-thousand miles on it? In 30 years, will you wish you had saved that money and protected your margin instead?"

Often, when we get to this point of the discussion, people realize that as nice as a new car would be, in 30 years they won't remember that new car smell. A

30-year perspective helps them see it's just another car. It will get them from point A to point B, but there's nothing about having the biggest, best, newest version that will change their lives. It's not worth overextending themselves with huge car payments, especially since this is just one of many cars they will have to purchase in that 30-year window. But that's not what happened in this particular instance.

Finney had been driving nothing but clunkers for 30 years, and always dreamed of owning a brand new muscle car. It was really the only selfish splurge he ever wanted. And Finney had been following a smart financial plan. So we looked at the math, decided to make a much larger down payment so it wouldn't impact his margin as much, and he bought the new car.

Did he lose out on some money that he could have saved? Sure he did. Was it worth it? Absolutely.

Tax Incentives: When Bad Math and Blinders Collide

One of my clients told me he had purchased a $50,000 piece of equipment for his company right at the end of the year so he could get the tax benefit.

"Do you need that piece of equipment? Are you going to use it?"

"No, I just wanted the tax write-off."

"So, did you just *really want* the new piece of equipment?"

"Not really."

"So you bought a $50,000 piece of equipment for the $14,000 tax benefit and the equipment is already worth only $35,000 because of depreciation. How does that math put you ahead?"

I see this kind of stuff all the time. One of the biggest problems with the tax code is it is designed to manipulate behavior. It is designed to incentivize certain choices and disincentivize and penalize other choices. In other words, the tax code serves as blinders that get us so focused on the potential tax benefit of a decision that we ignore everything else. Tax incentives exist to get you to fall in line, just like a horse pulling a carriage, and do the things the government wants you to do. When we don't realize we have these blinders on, we do things like buy a piece of equipment we don't need just because we get a big tax write-off, or get a giant mortgage that eliminates our margin just because the interest is deductible, or do a huge improvement on our house just because we get an energy credit.

Because tax incentives are designed to work as blinders, asking the two questions is a helpful exercise before purchasing anything for the tax write-off.

If there was no tax benefit involved, would you still put solar panels on your roof? Thirty years from now, will you care about whether or not you put solar panels on your roof?

If the answer is no, then doing it for the tax benefit won't make it a good financial decision. If the answer is yes, then you don't really need the tax benefit to justify the decision. The bottom line is that if the decision does not stand on its own without the tax benefit, it's probably not a good decision.

They Stand on Their Own

Good decisions *always* stand on their own.

One of the biggest reasons we think we have to justify every decision with math is because we worry about what other people think. Will they think I am being extravagant and selfish? Will they think I have no financial sense and I am just throwing my money away? As hard as it is to admit, we all care a little bit too much about what other people will think. But there are two ironies about using the math to justify our choices. The first is that others don't care about our decisions as much as we think they do. Most of your friends aren't worried about whether or not you made the best financial decision. They're just happy for you that you got a new car! The second irony is that people have more respect for us when we are honest about our motives.

"We spent the money because we really wanted grandchildren."

"I took a cut in salary because I wanted to enjoy my life and not die young."

"I bought the new car because it had been a dream of mine for 30 years!"

These decisions resonate with us on a human level. They don't need numbers to prove they have meaning.

When you work with a financial advisor, it's their job to help you take off your blinders when you're not seeing the big picture, or help clear out your smokescreen when you are trying to fool yourself or others, so that you can get to a decision that stands on its own. Sometimes that decision will be to play it safe, but every once in a while, that decision will be to swing for the fences. I hope you can use the two questions to help you know when life is giving you an opportunity to live a life that is uniquely rich for you. And, when it comes, I hope you swing hard.

CHAPTER 8

Let Your Kids Learn How to Handle Money

One of my newer clients came in recently, all stressed out, and said "I don't know what I'm going to do with my son,"

"What do you mean?" I asked.

"He just made his first major purchase on his own. He bought a car, and it's a piece of junk. It's already broken down twice in three weeks. I knew I should have gone with him to pick out the car. I could have saved him a lot of heartache. And money."

He paused and then talked about a deeper concern.

"My son is horrible with money. I have this dread in the pit of my stomach that I'm going to leave him all my money and he's going to blow through it in a couple of years. What should I do?" I wanted some clarification.

"You said this was his first major purchase on his own.

What else has he bought on his own?"

"Nothing, really," he replied. "He's never needed to buy anything. If he wanted something, I would buy it for him—if it was a good purchase. I always kept stuff like this from happening. And I was right, 'cause look at the boneheaded move he made right out of the gate. What's it going to take to turn this kid around?"

I thought seriously about it and did some quick mental calculations before answering.

"About 50 more boneheaded moves would be a good start," I said.

He looked confused. "Listen," I continued, "Your son bought a horrible car. He probably bought it for all the wrong reasons. He thought it would make him happy. He thought it would make him look cool. He didn't do enough research, whatever. It was a horrible buying decision. My son did the same thing last month. He bought a car with his own money that turned out to be a piece of junk. He also thought it was going to make him look cool. The only difference is my son is eight years old and the radio-controlled car he bought was only 50 bucks. But it's the exact same mistake. Your son's mistake just had more zeros and a comma attached to it."

He sat thinking about it and I pressed a little further. "What was the very first thing you bought with your own money?" I asked.

"A transistor radio," he said proudly. "I played that thing every day for years." Then he got a sheepish smile on his face. "The second thing I bought was a used bike. It was a yellow bike with a banana seat. I bought it from one of the older kids in school. It turned out to be a total piece of junk. I threw it in a dumpster two months later."

He sat there smiling, as though he was recalling a favorite memory.

"You know," he said, "that experience made a big impact on me."

"If you really want to help your son," I said, "tell him about the yellow bike."

The Power of Regret

Regret is a powerful teacher. The lessons that regret can teach us leave an indelible impression. Unfortunately, one of the most common mistakes parents make is keeping their kids from experiencing regret by not allowing them to make bad financial decisions. We know that the plastic piece of junk in the grocery store is going to break on the way home, so we don't allow them to buy it. That feels like a double success, because we didn't waste money and we prevented our children from experiencing disappointment.

But here's the problem: Mistakes are a natural and necessary part of the learning experience. Your kids fell down a few times before learning to walk. They fell down a few times before learning how to ride a bike. They will fall down more than a few times on their way to mastering financial decisions. Failure is not the opposite of success; it's part of the process of success. There is no forward progress without failure. You don't get to decide whether or not your children will make mistakes with money. You only get to decide if they make them while they are young and the price tag is small, or whether they make them when they are older, when the price tag can be staggering.

It might seem counter-intuitive, but here is the absolute truth when it comes to teaching your children about money: Your kids will never learn from the mistakes you don't let them make. Your kids will never learn from the successes you don't let them experience by making enough mistakes. When you take away the possibility of making mistakes and learning from them, you are taking away an essential condition for achieving financial aptitude.

Anatomy of a Learning Experience

It's not enough to allow your kids to make mistakes. You want to make sure that they learn from the mistakes. You want your home to be a laboratory, where you are setting up and controlling the financial experiments so that your kids gain insight from each new mistake. There are three essential components that have to be present in order for learning to occur.

The first component is the conversation before the purchase. This is where you help your kids figure out why they want to buy something. Why do they want it? Why do they think it will make them happy? What do they think it will do? What promise is this product making to them? Do they remember the last time they bought something kind of like this? Do they remember the flaw in it? Are they sure this one's different? What makes them so sure?" Your job in this conversation is not to give your kids the answers; it's simply to ask the questions that they need to think through for learning to occur. Here's an example:

"Dad, I want to get this rocket! It's really cool!"
"Oh yeah? What do you like about it?"

"You pump it up and it shoots, like, a hundred and fifty feet in the air!"

"A hundred and fifty feet? You sure about? That's pretty high."

"Yeah! Look at that picture!"

The second essential component of a learning experience is the kids must use their own money. To experience regret, a bad purchase needs to cost kids something. That can't happen if they are using your money. So, to make sure they are using their own money, I suggest you open up a branch of what I like to call The Bank of Mom and Dad.

In our home, The Bank of Mom and Dad is simply a spreadsheet that tracks each of our children's finances. If you search online for templates to set up a bank account register, you will find lots of free options you can use to set up your own version. Since we want our kids to learn how money works, we try to operate The Bank of Mom and Dad as close to a real bank as possible. We have paper checks that they can write to get money out of their account. We use reloadable debit cards because we want them to learn that even though it's easy to swipe that plastic, it's still being paid for — it's still coming out of their balance. When they get their allowance, they decide how much of it they want on their debit card, how much in cash, and how much they want to leave in the bank.

The Bank of Mom and Dad takes effort. Doing all the tracking can be a pain in the butt. But it's an investment in your kid's future, and it's well worth the effort because each of their mistakes actually costs them something.

"Can I get the rocket, Dad?"

"You have money. Is that something you think would make you happy? Is that something you would use? Is that something you would enjoy?"

"Yes."

"Let's find out. You buy it."

The third essential component of a learning experience is the conversation and empathy after the purchase: This is where you help your kids compare what they thought the purchase was going to mean to them to what it actually ended up meaning. It's also a time to empathize with their regret if they end up disappointed. So, after spending forty minutes exhausting himself pumping up the rocket and getting it to go no further than twelve feet in the air, your kid is regretting his purchasing decision:

"This rocket is lame!"

"Yeah, it's not going as high as you hoped it would,

"No! It doesn't do anything!"

"Man, that's frustrating. I remember in the store you said the picture made it look like it was going to go 150 feet in the air."

"It did! That picture was a total lie."

"I completely agree. That picture was a lie."

"They shouldn't be allowed to lie like that. That makes me mad."

"You're right, but a lot of those pictures are meant to make you think a toy will do something it really can't do. They're trying to trick you. It sure makes sense that you're angry about that."

Here's one of the cool things about allowing your kids to learn from their own mistakes: You can be on their side as they learn. If it was your money that they used to buy the rocket, if they wore you down after begging and crying, the natural thing to do after the rocket is a flop is to say, "I told you so! You should listen to me next time!"

But the only thing anybody learns from an "I told you so" is that mistakes aren't allowed. Even when you use the purchase as a learning experience, there are times that everything in you wants to say, "You didn't see that coming? Are you really surprised it didn't fly a hundred feet in the air? I saw that a mile away!" But if you can remember that they've never walked past this trap before, you can empathize with them while the regret teaches them a valuable lesson.

The conversation after the purchase is critical because it allows the regret to teach your child something specific. What was it about that thing you were most excited about? What hooked you? Where was the disappointment? If it did what they wanted but was poorly made and broke in a day, that's one lesson. If it didn't even do what the packaging suggested, that's another lesson.

One of the beautiful things about mistakes is if you pay attention, you always make new ones and so you are learning new lessons. I always tell my kids, "It's okay to make mistakes. Just try to make new ones."

Now that we know the three essential components of a learning experience, let's talk about the key areas where you need to help your kids learn how to handle money.

Buyer's Remorse

I want my kids to buy a tremendous number of useless pieces of plastic with their own money. I want this because I know that with those useless pieces of plastic, my kids will get to experience buyer's remorse, which is one of the most powerful financial teachers around. Buyer's remorse is the Yoda of financial wisdom — and the more time your children spend with Yoda when they are young, the less they will need him when they are older.

There are many different causes of buyer's remorse, and your kids will need to experience all of them several times on their journey to financial wisdom. Here are some of the major categories of buyer's remorse. As you read through the list, think about the price tag involved if the purchase is made when they are five or ten years old, and what the price tag would be if they made the mistake when they were 30-five. Don't be fooled — they are going to make each of these mistakes and feel each of these kinds of remorse:

- Remorse that comes from buying something on impulse instead of taking time to figure out if they really want or need it. At first, the giddy feeling of having their own money will lead to several experiences of this kind.

- Remorse that comes from buying something because the marketing made it look better than it was. This is a mistake kids will need to make several times, because there are so many ways advertising can hook us into poor buying choices.

- Remorse that comes from buying something that is cheaply made and breaks quickly.

- Remorse that comes from buying something because their best friend has it and they don't want to feel left out or inferior.

- Remorse that comes from buying something because it's the newest fad and everyone has it, and then realizing they don't like it and never use it.

- Remorse that comes from buying something without doing enough research, then realizing that they could have purchased a superior version for the same or less money.

- Remorse that comes from buying something without knowing themselves. They think that art set or that tennis racket looks fun, but then discover that they think art is kind of boring or that they hate playing tennis.

There is a learning curve that happens with each of these kinds of buyer's remorse, with lots of mistakes on the front end. But if you treat each of these mistakes as a learning experience, your kids will eventually learn powerful lessons. When I tell my kids that we're going to the store, my two youngest kids get wide-eyed and ask if they can buy something. They're still learning about impulse buying, so I tell them to bring their wallets. My oldest leaves his wallet at home, because he's learned that lesson.

There is another consequence that comes from allowing your kids to make their own mistakes: Sometimes the purchase you think will lead to regret turns out to be a really great purchase. One time, my son Wes wanted to buy a little toy out of one those bubble-gum machines that you put two-quarters in and crank the knob. He got a little plastic ball that opens up when you press a button. I'd have bet a million dollars that that fifty cent thing would have been worthless to him in five minutes — and he's had it for five years.

Wes carried that little plastic ball around for years, pretending it was a spaceship one day and a time machine the next day. Something about that little piece of plastic connected with his creativity and imagination. I discovered that he loves miniature gadgets that fit in his hand, or that he can keep in his pocket and take out to play with. At Christmas, we started giving him a little box of office supplies — rubber bands, paper clips, tape, etc. — and he spends hours creating the most amazing little miniatures with them. We wouldn't have known to give him that gift if he hadn't put two quarters in that stupid machine.

Every once in a while, a purchase that you think will be a lesson in buyer's remorse will instead give you insight into how your kids are uniquely wired. You will find your children enjoying something, and realizing it's because they are a burgeoning engineer, or architect, or storyteller, or artist. And you wouldn't have made that discovery if you hadn't allowed them to make their own choices.

Savings

One of the most powerful things you can teach your kids through The Bank of Mom and Dad is the power of saving. Please don't take your kids to a real bank and have them open up a children's savings account that pays 0.001% interest. What will they learn if they save money for what feels like a lifetime and get paid a nickel in interest? They'll learn that saving money is worthless. In a Bank of Mom and Dad savings account, you can determine the interest rate and make it more like investing in the real world. In our home, The Bank of Mom and Dad currently pays ten percent interest, and it might put us in the poor house the way our kids save! When your children see that their savings interest each month is as much as their allowance, they understand how powerful investing can be. I have a client that I told about The Bank of Mom and Dad idea years before I had kids. He started using it with his children and the first thing his daughter did when she got her first job was open a Roth IRA. She was fourteen years old at the time.

Needs First, and Then Wants.

A hallmark of financial maturity is learning to pay for your needs first, and then using what is left for the things you want. For kids to learn this at home, we have to slowly ask them to pay for some of the things they need out of their own account at The Bank of Mom and Dad. Here's how this works at our house. Each of our kids gets a weekly allowance based on their age — a dollar per year. So the eleven year-old gets eleven dollars a week, the eight year-old gets eight dollars a week, and so on. Each year, they get a one dollar raise. But with more money comes more responsibility to pay for things they need. The eleven year-old, for example, now has to buy his own shoes, while the younger kids don't. He knows he has to prioritize shoes over PlayStation games. Someday, he will have to pay a little bit of rent. By gradually giving your kids responsibility to pay for the things they need with their own money, you teach them that money isn't just for blowing. They learn how to have a spending plan even before they leave home.

Generosity

To really get the benefit of generosity, kids have to be giving away something that belongs to them. It's not enough to be part of a generous family, or to watch mom and dad being generous. That's a great start, but it doesn't cost them anything. When kids encounter the option to sacrifice some of their own money for someone else, the experience unlocks a ton of value. They feel all the benefits of a generous life, and they get to start when they're eleven.

One of my absolute favorite moments as a dad came from watching a completely unprompted act of generosity by my son Max. We were at his school's family fun night and Max and his friends walked up to me, all with root beer floats.

"Those look good," I said.

"Yeah," said one of Max's friends, "Max bought us all one!"

I was so proud of him for that spontaneous act of generosity, and from the look on his face I knew he had the sense of satisfaction that comes from being generous. That's an experience he can only have if he has his own money to spend.

Becoming Savvy Spenders

As your kids grow through each of these lessons, you can begin to build on those lessons by teaching them the best way to get what they want. For example, my son wanted an iPod Touch, and we told him he could buy it when he turned ten. On his tenth birthday, he was online, ready to make the purchase. I let him know that he could buy the same thing refurbished and save a bunch of money. He did some research and discovered he could save $80 by buying a used iPod, and that's what he did — even though he wasn't getting the free overnight shipping and had to wait a couple extra days to get it.

There is a lot of learning that has led to being able to make that kind of wise decision. He's learned about impulse buying, so he doesn't 't have to have the iPod overnight. He can wait a few more days. He is paying for some of his needs as well as wants, and he has a savings account — so he knows what eighty is worth. And, because he bought it with his own money — and he knows the value of his own money — he treats that iPod Touch well. He's had it for over a year and a half and it is still in mint condition. If I had been making all of his decisions, I would have bought the refurbished iPod for him and it would probably be broken or lost by now.

Credit Cards

You don't want your children learning how to handle credit cards after they leave home. When your kids go to college, credit card companies paint a huge target on their backs, because they know that most college age kids don't understand how credit works. They get in college and they blow six hundred dollars and they get a statement that says they owe twenty-five, and so that's what they pay. Those college kids will rack up a ton of debt and make the minimum payment, and the credit card companies will make an obscene pile of interest on them over the course of their lifetime.

I tell parents to get their kids a credit card as soon as they start driving. Have the kids use it only for gas, and have them pay it off every month. If they use it for anything else, it gets taken away. This way, your kids get used to how the billing cycle works. They're going to look at that monthly statement and see that the credit card company says they only owe $5, but they're going to pay off the entire balance.

Another benefit of doing this is your kids begin building a credit history. Because of this, I suggest that they get a national credit card, one that they will be able to keep even if they move far from home. If you get them a card from the local credit union and they switch it seven years from now for a more national card, they will lose those seven years of credit history. I have a Discover card that I've had since I was sixteen. When I graduated from college and went to buy my new first car, I got the lowest interest payment the bank offered, even though it was my first major purchase. I already had a strong credit history, and your kids can do the same thing.

It's Never Too Late to Allow Your Kids Experience Regret

The client I talked about at the beginning of this chapter thought it was his job to prevent his kids from making mistakes. Because of that, his son never learned from the mistakes his dad didn't allow him to make. When I told him the solution was for his son to make more bone-headed mistakes, as he called them, I was being absolutely serious. I wanted my client to understand this so we could avoid one of the most devastating regrets that people can experience.

The problem is not just that when your kids make mistakes as adults, the mistakes are going to have a bigger price tag attached to them. The problem is that those mistakes have the potential to do real, lasting damage to your relationship with your kids. When we don't allow our children to learn from trial and error when they're young, when we wait for the big, costly mistake, parents often feel the need to swoop in and rescue their kids. But it's not just swooping in a rescuing, it's swooping in and rescuing and making them feel like idiots.

"I can't believe you got into this mess!"

"Do you know what this is going to cost me to bail you out of this?"

"Are you ever going to grow up and start acting like an adult?"

I've seen parents and kids drift far apart because of a financial mistake that was made ten or fifteen years ago.

But it sets in motion the posture that "I'm never going to engage with my parents or rely on them for anything because they make me pay for it emotionally a thousand times over." And the parents become entrenched in the thought that "I'm never going to give them any of my resources because they're irresponsible." So I see these parents who have worked their whole lives to build their fortune and are not able to use it to bless the children *that they love.* And I see children who need help and guidance but are afraid to get it from the parents *that they love.*

It's heartbreaking to watch and so avoidable if we could just realize that trial and error are always a part of learning. If your kids learn to play the guitar at ten years old or at 30 years old, they're going to make the exact same mistakes. The same is true with learning how to handle money. I just spoke to a client whose children are going to inherit three-and-a-half million dollars, but he won't give them any money now because they will just blow it.

"Jerry," I said, "You're just doubling down on the same mistake. You didn't let them make mistakes when they would have cost fifty dollars. You're not allowing them to make mistakes now when the price tag is in the thousands. You're just going to wait until the mistakes cost hundreds of thousands of dollars. They're going to make mistakes. You can't control it. The only choice you have is if you're going to be on their side when they make them so that you can be part of the learning curve." At some point, we have to not only allow our kids to fail, but also allow them to experience the pain of regret that comes from failing while still being on their side.

I get it. It's hard to watch your kids struggle and hurt. It's especially hard to do it when you feel guilty that you didn't do enough to teach them how to make good financial decisions. Stepping in and bailing them out by paying off their debt or buying another car feels like the right thing to do. The problem is it is just perpetuating the same mistake, and preventing your kids from having a learning experience. I had some clients who agreed to give their son one thousand dollars a month to help bail him out of his overspending. They hated seeing how much anxiety it caused him. The problem was that once the anxiety was gone, he had no motivation to change and he used the thousand dollars to overspend even more.

As parents of older children we need to be able to distinguish between the times our kids are experiencing pain from a recoverable mistake, and when they are experiencing something truly devastating. If your kids have amassed three thousand dollars worth of credit card debt, it would be a whole lot easier to just bail them out. But three thousand dollars in credit card debt isn't going to kill anybody. Your kids can learn and grow from that mistake, and come out wiser on the other side.

If you struggle with continuing to rescue your kids from their mistakes, here's a place where you need to be honest with yourself. The regret that comes from not teaching your kids how to handle money is a twisty regret. Part of us loves it that our kids still need us. But that's something we are really doing for ourselves, not for our kids. My mom always said that the hardest part about being a mom is if you do it well you should work yourself out of a job. Her goal was that we would get to the point that we could do for ourselves all of the things that she was doing for us. She believes that is the test of a good mom. She's absolutely right.

None of us is born with financial brilliance. We all have to learn our lessons through the painful process of falling down and getting back up again. So relax. When your kids make a bad financial choice, the world is not coming to an end. Let them make mistakes. Let them make lots of mistakes. Talk to them about their purchases before they make them. Give them the opportunity to use their own money. And be there to empathize with them and talk through what they have learned. If you do that often enough, you will work yourself out of a job.

CHAPTER 9

Get a Trusted Advisor

In most areas in life, if you want to do something you've never done before the first step is to find a guide. You wouldn't want to parachute for the first time and just figure it out on your way down. You want an expert with lots of experience who can help you master the skill. Whether you want to learn to sail the ocean, climb Mt. Everest, or fly a plane, the first step is usually to find an expert. The one area of life where this is not the case is finances. A lot of people are convinced that they don't want or need a financial advisor.

I think the biggest reason many people don't want a financial advisor is the terrible reputation that the financial services industry has built up. In fact, it's my belief that the way the financial advice industry has marketed itself has caused not only its poor reputation, it has also caused people to look for the wrong things in a financial advisor. To understand what I mean, let me ask you two simple questions.

Would you like to know the secret to getting rich quick? Would you like to understand financial markets so thoroughly that you are always making money and never have a quarter where your investments dip?

Guess what? So would I! But that ain't happening.

What I want you to pay attention to, though, is the emotional reaction you had to those two questions. If you're like most people, you had (to some degree at least) two opposite reactions going on at once, and those reactions are at the heart of a real problem in the financial advice industry.

If you're like most people, there is a part of you that got a little excited by those questions. Your heart started beating a little faster. You leaned in a little bit and wondered, almost hoped, that someone had finally found the secret and was going to share it with you. How much would you pay for that knowledge? No price would be unreasonable if the secret delivered on its promises!

But, if you're like most people, there was another part of you that began to back away. Your guard went up. You've been around the block enough times to know there is no fountain of youth, no miracle cure for baldness, and no way to safely lose fifty pounds in a month. How much would you pay for the secret to get rich quick with no sacrifice and no downside? Nothing. Zilch. Zip. Because you know it doesn't exist.

And here is the credibility problem that the financial advice industry has created for itself, and why it has such a terrible reputation: for decades it has been marketing the secret. And as a result people have come to the conclusion that there is no way a financial advisor could ever justify his fee.

The reason the industry has been marketing the secret has a lot to do with human nature, and the difference between what we want as human beings and what we need. If we are honest with ourselves it's easy to recognize that what we want is to a quick, easy, and painless path to success. Who wouldn't want that? But if we are honest with ourselves we will also recognize that what we need is to live in reality. Here's the problem: it's a whole lot easier build your business quickly if you market to what people want rather than what people need. And the financial advice industry knows that there are three big things that people want.

First, they want to get rich quick. This is nothing new. I'm guessing that people have wanted to get rich quick about as long as people have been around. It would be nice to wake up next month with a large bank account without having to put in the time and effort required. That's why you'll hear lots of advertisements for fool-proof investments that promise crazy returns. But if that is the marketing, then a financial advisor is only valued if she can help you become a millionaire by next year, and that usually only happens when you win the lottery.

Secondly, people want to always make money without ever losing money. If we turn on the news and hear that the stock market has taken a dramatic down turn, we want to call our advisor and hear her say "Yeah, I saw that coming weeks ago. I moved all your investments, so you didn't lose a thing." That's why you'll even see some marketing that suggests if your investments take a downturn, then your advisor ought to work for free. But if that is the marketing then a financial advisor is only valuable if she can predict the future with certainty, or if she has control over whether the market goes up or down.

Thirdly, people want someone who will tell them what they want to hear. If they want to spend money on opulent cars and giant mansions, they want an advisor who will tell them that they can have a great future without sacrificing anything in the present. If they want to hoard all their money and never pay for shared experiences or give generously to others, they want to be told that they are being wise or prudent. That is why you will never hear an advertisement that says "come invest with us, because you're wrong so much more than you realize." Trust me, I've seen a lot of clients leave their advisors simply because the advisor had the audacity to challenge their thinking. But if that is the case, then your advisor is only valuable if you are always right, so why would you even need an advisor anyway?

So here's how all this plays out in the real world. Most of us know that getting rich overnight is unrealistic. But we wonder how fast is realistic. Most of us know we are going to have downturns at some point, but we wonder how much of a downturn is acceptable. Most of us know we are going to be wrong from time to time, so it is worth something to have someone to help us see the truth, but how much? Between the ridiculous "I'll pay anything to learn the secret" and the absurd "I'm always right so I don't need an advisor" we need to figure out how an advisor would justify her fee. And this is what we do: between one extreme and the other we pick a completely arbitrary, random rate of return point and boil down an advisor's worth based on their ability to hit that benchmark.

Why do we pick a random rate of return point? Because we believe we need something to measure. We need something to quantify. Arbitrary or not, now we have a way to evaluate the advisor's performance.

But this is the exact wrong way to value a financial advisor, for two big reasons. The first reason is we are still thinking in the wrong categories. We are still thinking in categories created by catering to our unrealistic wants instead of what we really need. It's like we're saying "I know my advisor can't be a genie, but if he can be this close to being a genie, then he's valuable."

The second reason is because the rate of return is the one thing your financial advisor has the least control over. Markets go up, and markets go down. That's what they do. You've heard the saying that a rising tide lifts all boats. That's the way it works in the world of investments as well. Financial planners can help steer the ship, but no human can control the ocean. There are so many factors at play in the market that no one can predict with certainty what is going to happen or to what degree. The truth of the matter is that most of that stuff is commoditized now, anyway. You can go online and buy an asset allocation fund and you're pretty much done. It's not going to be as good, but it's not going to hurt you.

The real value of a financial planner lies in a completely different direction.

It's Groundhog Day!

In the movie *Groundhog Day* Phil Connors is forced to live the same day over and over again until he finally becomes the best version of himself and makes the most of his day. At first he thinks he is cursed, but it ends up being a wonderful opportunity. Phil is able to transform himself from a shallow, self-centered person who is isolated from everyone he meets, to a thoughtful, caring person who is one of the most beloved men in town. It's a striking difference, almost as if the Phil at the beginning of the movie and the Phil at the end of the movie are two completely different people: Miserable Phil and Contented Phil.

Contented Phil has a huge advantage over Miserable Phil, however, and it is this: every decision that Miserable Phil is about to make for the first time, Contented Phil has already made hundreds of times. He has had the chance to see the outcomes every possible choice. At every fork in the road, Contented Phil knows which option leads to happiness, meaning and fulfillment, and which options seem good but lead to emptiness and regret. He's been there before. Many times.

Phil Connors is a perfect illustration of the true value of having a financial counselor. It's not about picking the right stocks. It's not about finding a secret method to get rich quick. The true value of a good financial advisor is this: every time you face a financial fork in the road for the first time, your advisor has already lived through that experience vicariously through his clients hundreds of times. A good advisor knows which option leads towards the life you told him you want to live and the goals you want to achieve, and which options lead to struggle and regret. He has been there before. Many times.

When you are deciding when to retire for the first and only time it would be nice, like Phil Connors, to have the option of do-overs. That way, if you retire too early and end up struggling financially, or if you retire too late and waste years you could have spent enjoying friends and family, you could just go back and make a different choice. But unlike Contented Phil we don't get do overs. We often get one shot at making the right choice, and there's a lot hanging in the balance.

In chapter eight we talked about how helpful it is to learn from our mistakes when we are young and the price tag isn't devastating. This is the flip side of that coin. When we are older and we have one shot at a major decision — and no do-overs — we don't want to have to learn from our mistakes. The cost is way too high, and the impact on our lives and the people we love is too important.

When you are deciding when to retire it's the very first time you've faced that decision. But I've faced it 683 times with 683 clients. I've seen all the different ways that decision can be made. Because of that, I can walk you through that fork in the road with confidence. I can say, "I've seen this movie before. In fact, I've seen it with forty-three different endings. I can tell you which decisions led to an ending full of regret, and which decisions led to the ending you've told me you wanted. So I can tell you if you retire now you are not going to have the kind of retirement you told me you want." Or, "You can retire with confidence today. You're ready."

Think about some of the financial questions we all have to answer at some point: When and how should I start saving for my children's college expenses? Can I afford to take this lower paying job that would be more life-giving? Do I have what I need to start my business? Is this the right time to sell my business? How much will I need for retirement, and what's the best way to get there? Here's what these and many other financial decisions have in common: we won't experience the full impact of them for ten, twenty, even fifty years. That's a long time to wait to see if you made the right choice. To have someone who has seen all the different ways the movie can end and can tell us which decision led to which ending is priceless.

In my years as a financial advisor, I've come to understand Phil Connors. I've come to realize that the reason he was able to go from being Miserable Phil to Contented Phil isn't just because he had a lot of do-overs. The reason he was able to change so much is because, over time, he becomes more and more connected with what he really wants. But he does that by feeling the pain of the mistakes that he has made.

I've felt that with my clients, and that is why I'm so passionate about the subject of money and regret. I had a client who kept delaying his retirement. Year after year I told him he was ready to retire.

"Go now."

"No, maybe next year. If I stay another year I'll get a bonus."

"You don't need the bonus. You have enough. Go now."

But every year he put it off. Then, in the year he finally decided to retire he was diagnosed with cancer and died within the year. He and his wife never got to do any of the things that they dreamed of doing. It was gut wrenching to watch.

There is a big difference between what is hypothetical and what is real. When you are going into retirement for the first and only time, the idea that you might die before enjoying retirement is merely hypothetical.

"Sure, it could happen, but that bonus I'll get if I work three more years is pretty big."

For me it's not hypothetical. It's not something that could happen; it's something that has happened. I've seen the impact on the widow and family. I've seen the pain and the regret.

It's not just intellectual with me. It's visceral. This is what financial advisors deal with. What we experience when we see clients go through really hard stuff is life-altering. It becomes part of who we are. And we want to help our clients avoid that pain and regret with every ounce of our being. That is the real value of a good financial advisor.

Finding the Right Advisor for You

In looking for the right advisor, the first step is to do a search for a Certified Financial Planner, or CFP. A CFP is to financial planning what a CPA is to accounting: you have to pass a board exam that demonstrates a wide breadth of knowledge in your field. It's not an easy designation to get. You can go to the CFP board and you will find a directory of Certified Financial Planners in your area.

The CFP designation is a good starting point, but it's not enough. You wouldn't want someone to perform your heart surgery just because they've read a book and passed a test. You also want someone who has a lot of successful experience. In order to see who has the right experience, you will have to interview a few of them.

The way the interview is held will tell you a lot. If you walk into a meeting with a financial advisor and they have a sixty minute presentation on how big they are, how many clients they have, and how much money they manage, then you're in the wrong place. If they move quickly to a particular financial product they think you should buy, or answer a question that you are not asking, that's all the warning you should need to go someplace else. They're not interested in what matters, they're only interested in making a sale.

But if you walk into a meeting and they want to talk about you, then steer the conversation to things like "how many times have you seen people in my situation. Tell me some stories. What are some of the mistakes you've seen people make? What are some of the successes?" Their answers to these questions will help you see if they have had the experience you want. It will also help you see if they agree with you in your philosophy of what matters and what is important. If all they do is tell stories about how someone could have saved more, they might not be seeing the big picture.

Saving more isn't what always what prevents real regret. Saving more doesn't always lead to a richer life. In this conversation you are starting to test if you are going to have real conversations about life, or if you are just going to talk about numbers getting bigger. If they never get out of the numbers, they're never going to provide the coaching and confidence you need to live a rich life.

The final suggestion I would make as you interview is to look for someone who can serve as a quarterback for your team. The problem in this industry is most of the time people come at these financial questions in these siloed approaches. You have an accountant over here and an attorney over there, you've got four different places money is invested and they never talk to each other. And they each have their own idea about what is important. The tax person says the most important thing is to never pay taxes (because that's how he proves his value) and the attorney says the most important thing is that we complicate stuff (that's how he justifies himself and charges hourly rates). And the investment guys think the most important thing is to beat some arbitrary benchmark (because that's how you know they're good at what they do). But none of those people are talking about what really matters, which is what you want out of life, and none of them are talking to each other.

You need a CFP who can make sure everyone is on the same page, because they get the whole picture. And, because they understand how everything works together, they can lead the team of accountants and attorneys in a coordinated effort to get the best results.

The Right Focus

When you have found a financial planner who is competent and experienced, and who can serve as your quarterback, the final thing to look for is a planner who is focused on the right things: knowing you, reminding you, and challenging you.

It starts with knowing you. I train my team that when they go into a prospect meeting they should be able to present our value proposition in ninety seconds or less; then spend the balance of the time talking about the customer. There is no one-size fits all life. If we don't get to know what our customers want out of life, what challenges they are facing, and what their values, hopes and dreams are, we have absolutely no value to add. All of the learning and experience in the world is only help-ful if your advisor takes the time to get to know what you want your story to look like.

Take the Plunge

The second thing you want from your financial plan-ner is to remind you of the promises you made to your younger self, and to give you the courage to keep them. This is one of the big surprises of my career. I think I just assumed that when people get to the point that they could live out their dreams, they would take the plunge. But that's not usually the case. You will not naturally have the courage to do something that you've never done before. Someone has to put that courage in you. I've been surprised by how often people need someone to say "I'm an expert in this, I've seen this a hundred times, and you should absolutely take this step." Then, not only are they able to take the plunge, they are able to take it fearlessly.

You don't want a financial planner that is perfectly willing to let your money sit in a pile and get bigger and bigger while you are missing out on the opportunities to live out your dreams. Tell your advisor the promises you made to your younger self, and ask them to hold you accountable if it looks like you're going to break those promises. Ask them to give you the courage to take the plunge when the time is right.

The Question on Everyone's Lips

The final thing you need in an advisor is someone who is willing to challenge you. Let's go back to *Groundhog Day* for a moment. In the movie, Phil Connors is at a loss to explain why he keeps living the same day over and over. He has no idea what he needs to do to escape his unending cycle. Interestingly, he is given a clue each and every morning. Do you remember what the radio announcers proclaim at the start of every day? The big question on everyone's lips is "will Phil see his shadow." That's the key. Phil has a shadow, and it is preventing him from becoming the best version of himself and making the most of his day.

We all have a shadow that is preventing us from living the life we want, and one of the places our shadow does its biggest damage is in our finances. For some of my clients, their shadow is acting out of worry. Every time there is a blip in the market they want to over-react and sell everything. I often joke that if all I do with some of my anxiety prone clients is take their phone calls and tell them to stay the course, I have earned my salary a thousand times over. For others, their shadow is the lure of more, or the lie of being irreplaceable. These clients are tempted over and over to trade relationship for money.

Other clients' shadow is fearing that they will never have enough, and so they can miss opportunities to be generous. For others, their shadow the denial that bad things will ever happen, so they can miss how important it is to prepare for the worst. Each of the chapters of this book describes a shadow that could prevent you from having the life you want. Find the chapter that resonates with you the most, and find an advisor who can help you see your shadow. The regret you will avoid if you do this one thing is life altering.

We all have shadows, but it's really hard to see our own shadows and how they are impacting our decisions. I'm pretty good at my job, but I have a financial advisor because I know I don't always see my shadow. We all need someone whose job it is to tell us the hard truth about ourselves. If you don't have a relationship with an advisor that you trust to challenge you, you're not going to get very far.

Get Started

The sooner you start with a financial advisor, the easier it is to get to where you want to go in life. If you start when you are twenty years old, the sacrifice you need to make to get where you want to go is comically small. If you wait until you're forty, it's a whole lot harder. Most people don't find us until they're fifty. But it's never too late.

I truly hope you get the opportunity to live a rich life. For that to happen, you need to discover what matters most to you — what will make your life rich.

You will also need the confidence to fearlessly pursue the things that are most important to you and not worry about all of the things that can get in the way.

But you can't do that alone. You need a seasoned, experienced expert in your corner.

You need a coach who will help you know yourself, who will remind you to keep the promises that you made to your younger self, and who will challenge your shadow whenever necessary. With the right advisor on your side, you can avoid so much needless regret, and you can live a rich life while building and spending your fortune.

Acknowledgments

This book would not have happened without the help and encouragement of so many people. I have more people to thank than I could list here, but I would like to highlight a few.

My incredible wife, Amy. Yet another one of my harebrained ideas that you have believed in. You are my biggest cheerleader and encourager. You have supported me in everything I do no matter how crazy it seems. You give me confidence when I need it, and help to bring me back to earth when I get full of myself. It is an honor and a delight to share this life with you.

Greg Williams. You have made the stories in this book come to life. You helped me tap into the emotion and the heart of how we deal with money. It is what sets this book apart. You are a brilliant writer and a wonderful friend. Sharing this project with you has been a true joy.

My mom. You were the first person to tell me I should write a book years ago. I laughed it off. Like so much of what you have said to me over the years, you ended up being right. Thank you for telling me so often that I can do anything I put my mind to. You have always been more confident in me than I am. Thank you for believing in me. And, congratulations on working yourself out of a job. Mostly.

My dad. I feel like no matter what I do, you will tell everyone you know that I am amazing. Making you proud of me has been a lifelong goal. Knowing you always are proud of me no matter what is deeply satisfying. Thank you for your love and encouragement.

My clients. The stories in this book are an amalgamation of hundreds of clients that I have worked with over the years. Through almost 20 years of walking through life with my clients, I have had the privilege of gleaning wisdom from all of them as they do their best to live a rich life. Some of what I have seen has been terribly hard and deeply painful, and much of it has been beautiful and sweet. All of it has been incredibly valuable. It has been an honor to be a part of all of your lives. Thank you for inviting me in and being in a relationship with me. I do not take what I have learned for granted. Your lives have been a tremendous gift to me.

About the Authors

James Lenhoff is a graduate of Miami University with a degree in marketing. A CERTIFIED FINANCIAL PLANNER™, he worked in financial planning with a large national firm before helping to found Wealthquest Corporation in 2006. He helped build the company on a model of comprehensive, long-term service to clients. Married and the father of three, James spends much of his free time on service projects through his church, including financial literacy education programs, and mission work in Haiti.

G.E. Williams is a graduate of Cincinnati Christian University and the author of *How to Use Your Heart: A Practical Guide to Loving Well.* He is the founder of Next Level Freedom, a community that helps people develop healthy relationships. He and his wife, Valerie, love to hang out with friends and cheer for the Lakers, Bengals, and Buckeyes.

Author Contact Information

James M. Lenhoff, CFP®
President, Wealthquest Corp.
50 E-Business Way, Suite 120
Cincinnati, Ohio 45241
513.530.9700
jlenhoff@wqcorp.com
www.wqcorp.com

Follow Living a Rich Life book news and events at Facebook.com/LRLBook

Additional copies of this book may be purchased at Amazon.com, Braughlerbooks.com, and select bookstores in Greater Cincinnati. To contact the author for speaking engagements or book signings, see above.

CPSIA information can be obtained
at www.ICGtesting.com
Printed in the USA
FFHW010857240219
50632491-56026FF